T0214124

Introduction to Scientific Visualization

Helen Wright

Introduction to Scientific Visualization

Helen Wright, MA, DPhil
Department of Computer Science
University of Hull
Hull
UK

British Library Cataloguing in Publication Data
A catalogue record for this book is available from the British Library

Library of Congress Control Number: 2006927788

ISBN-10: 1-84628-494-5   Printed on acid-free paper
ISBN-13: 978-1-84628-494-6

9 8 7 6 5 4 3 2 1

Springer Science+Business Media, LLC
springer.com

To Mike

Preface

About This Book

This book was first suggested to Springer in 2004, though its origins go back to changes made two years earlier to the structure of the University of Hull's Computer Science programme. At the same time, my own visualization research was leading towards a systematic view of data and techniques that I felt could be educationally valuable. In 2003 I thus sat down with some trepidation to write a visualization course founded on research in the area but nonetheless accessible to students. This course could, however, involve no mathematics beyond GCSE, in line with university admissions practices of that time. Writing the course involved generating many new illustrations, in the form of both line drawings and visualization screenshots and, wishing to get maximum mileage out of this effort, the idea of writing a book to accompany the course came about.

At the University of Hull, our practical visualization teaching is based on IRIS Explorer, an application builder-type package from NAG Ltd. Originally this book was to have been both an introduction to visualization *and* a handbook for beginners in IRIS Explorer, with 'virtual laboratories' running throughout it to illustrate certain points. Following comments from reviewers, however, its emphasis has changed. Most of the screenshots and all of the colour plates are attributable to IRIS Explorer, but explanatory material is presented in general terms without reference to any particular package; the virtual laboratories comprise some of the example problems confined to the ends of certain chapters. The necessary IRIS Explorer software to tackle the problems on Windows(TM) machines is hosted on Springer's web site; go to http://www.springer.com/1-84628-494-5 to download the files you will need. If you are not an IRIS Explorer user, you can find out about it at http://www.nag.co.uk/Welcome_IEC.asp. Trial copies that will run for a month – more than enough time to complete the problems – are available.

Although the software in support of the problems presently caters just for IRIS Explorer users, the phrasing of the problems and their solutions in the text is, I hope, sufficiently general to allow supporting software in other packages to be contributed at a later date. Needless to say, the publisher and I would be very pleased to hear from other teachers of visualization using different packages who might in due course wish to contribute complementary software to support the problem and solution set used in this book. Lecture slides to accompany the book are also available from http://www.springer.com/1-84628-494-5. Contact Springer on 00800 777 46437, or via their Web site, to obtain a token that will give you access.

In order to achieve a balance between scholarship and pragmatism, and bearing in mind that this is an introductory book, I took the decision not to cite the literature throughout the text. Instead, there is a chapter devoted to further reading which goes through the material I draw upon. Certain references that I believe are key to the subject are included there, but I make no pretence that this chapter describes the state-of-the-art, since the references span more than three decades of research. As such it is simply a record of work which I have found useful whilst trying to draw together the various concepts. The chapter describing software should be viewed likewise – inclusion or omission of any particular package should not be regarded as significant, rather it is those I have met myself which are mentioned.

Acknowledgments

My first professional encounter with scientific visualization was in 1990 when I joined the GRASPARC (GRAphical environment for Supporting PARallel Computing) project at the University of Leeds, under the direction of Ken Brodlie. I learned a great deal in the ensuing seven years; Ken's abiding interest in visualization accuracy has undoubtedly been influential for me and is an aspect that I hope comes across strongly in this book. Ken's support both at Leeds and since is deeply appreciated.

Once at Hull, I leaned heavily on Graham Kirby's pedagogical experience. Graham helped me to climb the steep learning curve of learning and teaching and I continue to be grateful to this day for his assistance.

A number of other people deserve special mention: Brian Ford, Steve Hague, Robert Iles, Jeremy Walton, and many others at NAG Ltd have been unfailingly supportive from even before the Leeds years; I am very grateful to Mike Brayshaw, Toby Howard, and Jeremy Walton for reading drafts of this work; Bill Crum, Tim David, Gary Griffin, Mike Johnson, Casey Leedom, Andy Sleigh, Astrid van Maanen, Jeremy Walton, and Jason Wood donated or prepared data used in the screenshots. Teaching visualization without any examples would be difficult indeed, and grateful thanks are due to all those in the IRIS Explorer community and beyond for their contributions over the years. Any omissions from this list of data credits are regretted and if notified will gladly be rectified in future editions. David Duce was the unwitting provider of the shares example in Chap. 2 – until the ontology workshop in

Edinburgh in 2004 I had struggled to think up an everyday instance of discontinuous, ordinal data.

As my publishers, Helen Callaghan and Catherine Brett of Springer, London, have been extraordinarily patient in the face of my novice author's queries. Frank Ganz and Allan Abrams of Springer, New York, have respectively provided valuable technical advice and production know-how.

Finally the most heartfelt thanks of all must go to my partner Michael Johnson, who simultaneously acts as technical expert, friend, supporter, and house-husband extraordinaire. Without him, this book, had it been completed at all, would have been written hungry and naked as the food and clean clothes ran out – a truly frightening thought for all who know me. Cheers, Mike!

York

Helen Wright
April 2006

Contents

Preface VII
  About This Book VII
  Acknowledgments VIII

1   Introduction 1

2   Potential and Pitfalls 7
  2.1 Understanding Data 7
      2.1.1 Using Space 8
      2.1.2 Using Colour 16
      2.1.3 Using Animation 17
  2.2 Misunderstanding Data 19
      2.2.1 Using the Right Tool for the Right Job 19
      2.2.2 The Perils of Interpolation 22
  Problems 25

3   Models and Software 27
  3.1 A Dataflow Model of Visualization 27
  3.2 Visualization Scenarios 30
      3.2.1 Computational Steering 30
      3.2.2 Distributed and Collaborative Visualization 31
  3.3 Visualization Software 33
      3.3.1 Historical Context 33
      3.3.2 Current Approaches 33
  Problems 36

4   Colour in Scientific Visualization 37
  4.1 The Electromagnetic Spectrum 37
  4.2 Colour Perception 38
  4.3 Modelling Colour 40
      4.3.1 RGB Colour Model 40

4.3.2 HSV Colour Model 41
4.3.3 Relating RGB and HSV 44
4.4 Mapping Data to Colours................................. 46
4.4.1 Nonlinear Colour Mapping 47
4.4.2 'Linear' Colour Mapping 48
4.4.3 Perceptual Effects and Colour Vision Deficiency 50
Problems 54

5 **Choosing Techniques** 55
5.1 Classifying Data... 55
5.1.1 Dependent and Independent Variables 55
5.1.2 Data Domain 58
5.1.3 Scalar and Vector Types 60
5.2 Taxonomy of Visualization Techniques 64
Problems 68

6 **Visualizing Scalars**...................................... 69
6.1 1D Data 69
6.1.1 Bar Chart, Pie Chart, and Scatterplot 69
6.1.2 Histogram and Line Graph 72
6.2 2D Data 73
6.2.1 2D Bar Chart 73
6.2.2 2D Histogram................................... 75
6.2.3 Bounded Region Plot 76
6.2.4 Image Display 76
6.2.5 Making a Framework 78
6.2.6 Contour Plot 81
6.2.7 Surface View 84
6.2.8 Height-field Plot 87
6.3 3D Data 90
6.3.1 Reduction to 2D 90
6.3.2 Isosurface 93
6.3.3 Volume Render 98
Problems 102

7 **Visualizing Vectors** 103
7.1 Arrow Plot 104
7.2 Streamline and Timeline 106
7.3 Streamribbon, Streamsurface, and Streamtube 108
7.4 Time Surface 110
7.5 Flow Texture 112
7.6 Unsteady Flow 112
Problems 115

8 **Bibliography and Further Reading**........................117

References 125

Solutions 129

Useful Information 135
    Web Sites 135
    Abbreviations 136
    Definitions 138

Index 145

1

Introduction

Visualisation as a human activity predates computing by hundreds of years, possibly thousands if we include cave paintings as examples of Man's attempts to convey mental imagery to his fellows. Visualisation specifically in the service of science has a rather shorter but distinguished history of its own, with graphs and models produced by hand all having been used to explain observations, make predictions, and understand theories.

The current era of visualisation, however, is different in its pace and spread, and both can be attributed to the modern invention of the computer. Today, we are bombarded with visual imagery – no news report is considered complete without flying in graphs of statistics; the weather report can be seen to animate rain-drop by rain-drop; our banks send us plots of our incomings and outgoings in an attempt to persuade us to manage our finances more responsibly.

Moreover, everyone can now produce their own computer graphics, with easy-to-use software integrated into word-processors that makes charts and plots an obligatory element of any report or proposal. More specialist packages in turn offer complex techniques for higher dimensional data. These used to be the domain of experts, but without the expert on hand to advise on their usage we run the risk of using the computer to make clever rubbish.

Visualisation has thus become ubiquitous. As a tool it is powerful but not infallible; this book will try to give an insight into both facets.

What Is Scientific Visualization?

The discipline of visualization[1] in scientific computing, or ViSC as it is sometimes abbreviated, is widely recognised to have begun in the 1980s, its birth

---

[1] Much early work took place in the USA and the adoption of the 'z' spelling, even in the UK, is a consequence of these origins. The remainder of this book will use this spelling.

marked by the production of a key report for the US National Science Foundation (NSF). Interest in visualization was stimulated by the happy coincidence of a number of factors. Workstations had become powerful enough to display graphics on the scientist's desktop and algorithmic developments were making the treatment of large datasets tractable. Figure 1.1 is typical of the output of modern scanning equipment that creates many megabytes of data per subject. Crucially, supercomputers could now run simulations of complex phenomena and produce more data than could otherwise be assimilated. Figure 1.2 shows the complicated pattern of flow within a double-glazing panel, computed for a particular temperature differential across it. The NSF report argued that continuing piecemeal computer graphics provision was tantamount to a waste of these compute resources.

Visualization thus owes much to computer graphics but is distinctive from it. Quite how depends on your view of computer graphics – for some people this term conjures up scenes of the sort we see in computer games or films about virtual reality. The aim here is to make the experience seem as real as possible, whether the scene depicted is imagined or taken from life. The elements used to draw such a scene – coloured polygons that can be rotated and translated – are just as much a part of the latter stages of visualization, but the pictures that are drawn in visualization are of abstract objects that represent data, not experiences. For others, 'computer graphics' will already be synonymous with the pictorial representation of data but, again, 'visualization' implies a difference in the degree to which the user can intervene. Visualization as it

Fig. 1.1. Modern scanning equipment can create many megabytes of data. Processing and displaying it at interactive rates was one of the challenges identified by the NSF report. Image credit: IRIS Explorer, test data suite.

was conceived in the 1980s is thus an interactive process to understand what produced the data, not just a means to present it.

This Book's Aims and Objectives

This book aims to give readers a start in the field of scientific visualization. Someone who works all the way through it (and better still, is able to tackle all of the problems that are set) will be equipped to choose appropriately and apply safely a set of basic techniques to some commonly occurring data types. It also aims to provide a stepping stone to other literature that might not be immediately accessible to someone new to the subject. In particular and given its introductory nature, this book does not treat unsteady flows comprehensively nor does it deal with tensor data.

This book doesn't intend to promote any particular type of package or software. Rather, it tries to demonstrate the range of available approaches to look for when trying to choose a package for oneself or one's client. As was mentioned in the Preface, the section on software is by no means exhaustive, and there are other packages available that are not covered here. The principles illustrated by means of the software that *is* described should, however, simplify the decision-making process when other products are considered.

All of the company and product names mentioned in Sect. 3.3 are trademarks or registered trademarks and are hereby acknowledged. Other trademarks are noted where they appear in the text.

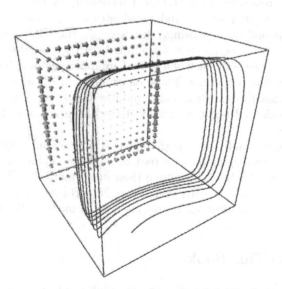

Fig. 1.2. Computer simulations can be 'fire hoses' of data that we cannot hope to understand without visualization. Image credit: IRIS Explorer, test data suite.

This Book's Assumptions

Although this book uses no mathematics itself, the concepts and explanations will be made easier to grasp by having studied mathematics to GCSE level or beyond. The book makes no assumptions about visualization or computer graphics other than as they are experienced by everyone at school. It should thus be accessible to someone starting out in the subject, but I hope it will also be interesting to readers who do have advanced mathematical skills and perhaps have already ventured into visualization. Using a taxonomic approach I have tried to show relationships between different data types and techniques, presenting an overview of the subject but treating it as a whole. Readers who are very experienced in visualization might therefore find the time spent on 1D and 2D data to be excessive compared with 3D, which is where a lot of the literature tends to dwell.

Who Should Read This Book?

Following its research origins in the 1980s and 1990s, visualization is now becoming commonplace; techniques are taught at undergraduate level in computer science that previously were considered specialist or confined to postgraduate theses. Science graduates are now expected to produce their own visualizations of complex data, when only a few years ago they would have enlisted the help of their computer centre or supervisor.

These two groups form the intended readership of this book. Primarily it is aimed at computer science undergraduates who are taking visualization as an advanced option. Increasingly (at least, in the UK), AS- or A2-level mathematics is not a requirement for admission to a computer science or informatics course, hence the lack of a formal approach here which some experts in the field will find surprising. Those on graphics MSc courses that include an element of visualization should also find it a useful overview before moving on to more specialised texts, especially if they have not met the subject as undergraduates.

Undergraduates and new postgraduates in science and engineering disciplines who need to display data as part of a course module or their project work can also use this book. Although their mathematical skills will outstrip what is presented here, there are nonetheless important approaches described that are worth assimilating before moving on to a more challenging text.

How to Use This Book

For someone with no prior experience, this book is best read from one end to the other (preferably from front to back), though the further reading can be left until later if time is short. If you have the necessary software, then either tackle the problems along the way or return to them chapter by chapter after first reading all the way through. Do try to tackle them *before* looking at the solutions as it is sometimes just as instructive to know why we found a problem difficult, as to be able to solve it. Unfortunately, looking first at the solution channels the mind into finding answers, rather than asking questions. If you don't have the specific software to support the problems, at least try to get hold of *some* software to try out the techniques – a lot of good software of the various types described in Sect. 3.3.2 is freely available. As the section *What is Scientific Visualization?* describes, understanding data is an interactive process, so doing visualization whilst reading about it will be far better than just seeing the words go by.

Those with some experience needn't read the book cover to cover. Candidates for skipping are the section on software in Chap. 3 and the descriptions of colour models in Chap. 4. If you are completely confident that you know what technique applies to what data[2] then skip Chap. 5. Try to resist the temptation to 'dip in' to Chap. 6 to find out about techniques for higher dimensions, without having read the earlier sections there. You might feel it is all revision, but a number of points are made for 1D and 2D data that are expanded upon later for 3D. If you are only interested in visualizing vectors then you can skip to Chap. 7 but might need to look at Chap. 4 to understand the rôle of colour and Sects. 6.2.5 and 6.3.1 in Chap. 6 if you haven't met triangulation.

---

[2] Ask yourself if you know the difference between a surface view and an isosurface. I find this is the litmus test that tells me what students have absorbed of the underpinning material.

2

Potential and Pitfalls

Any new technology brings both benefits and dangers, and scientific visualization is no different. Chapter 1 hinted at the insights to be gained using visualization, but there are always risks associated with any procedure that processes or transforms data. Richard Hamming famously said, "The purpose of computing is insight not numbers," but trouble lies in wait for us as soon as the numbers leave the safety of their data file to be turned into an insightful visualization. Incorrect assumptions about the properties of the data or its source, together with the complexities of the human visual system, can lead us to make representations that might mislead as much as they inform. This is recognised as a serious issue – for some years now the IEEE Visualization conferences, a premier forum for researchers in visualization, have begun with a 'VizLies' session, the purpose of which is to alert the community to these possibilities. An introductory book such as this cannot attempt to catalogue the diverse cases, successful and not, that appear at such a prestigious gathering. I hope, however, that a few well-chosen examples will serve both to encourage and to caution.

2.1 Understanding Data

Chapter 1 briefly introduces the notion of scientific visualization, placing it within the wider context of computer graphics. One factor described there was the often abstract nature of visualization, compared with the tendency in computer graphics to try to reproduce realistic scenes, whether imaginary or not. Although at first sight a contrast, this comparison in fact reveals one of the reasons why visualization is successful.

In computer graphics we employ various tricks, including perspective projection, hidden line and surface removal, and possibly stereographic images, to present a scene that fools our visual system into perceiving a space, or volume, drawn on the obviously flat computer screen. If, rather than using a workstation, we look at the scene within a virtual reality headset such that our head movement controls the viewpoint, we can add motion parallax to the list of cues which help us to perceive depth, even though the display in front of us is really nothing more than an array of coloured dots. Harnessing our innate understanding of space in order to generate insight into data is a fundamental aim of visualization. Unfortunately though, we are three-dimensional beings who inhabit a three-dimensional space. Our understanding of higher dimensions, other than the special case of time, is limited, so our visualizations will fundamentally be restricted to three dimensions, possibly including animation. If we have more variables to show than can be accommodated within this limited scope, we must resort to using colour, sound, and, most recently, force feedback. The next sections show in general terms what to be aware of when using space, colour, and animation to understand data. The use of other senses in scientific visualization (sometimes given the more general name 'perceptualisation') is still a research issue beyond the scope of this book. Datasets with very many variables are the domain of information visualization rather than scientific visualization and the reader is referred instead to one of a number of excellent texts that are available on this topic.

2.1.1 Using Space

One facet of understanding space, the cue of perspective, works hand in hand with an ability to compare the sizes of objects, whether present or remembered. Thus, when we see a familiar object such as a tree on the horizon we use our general knowledge of trees to attribute its apparently small size to its distance from us, rather than making the assumption we are looking at a nearby, but cleverly posed, bonsai. Of course, it might be just that, and we are all familiar with the trick camera shot of a model village which looks completely real until someone's knees appear! When ambiguity is removed though, we have a strong sense of relative object size, especially if the differences are not too great. Thus, in Fig. 2.1 we easily see that alternate bars are about half the height of their fellows but in Fig. 2.2(a) most of us would have difficulty judging the crop of smaller bars to be about one-tenth of the size of the larger. This becomes much easier, however, with the help of the gridlines that have been added in Fig. 2.2(b). Provided differences are distinguishable we also perceive extreme values readily – in Fig. 2.3 the lowest and highest values in the dataset are immediately obvious but it requires a moment's thought to sort the remainder.

Implicit in this discussion has been a natural tendency to associate greater value with larger objects and vice versa, without which the discipline of scientific visualization would in any case be a nonstarter. At first sight this is a reasonable assumption. For instance, I can climb a small mountain one day and a much bigger one the next; the exertion of getting to the top will obviously be greater on the second day. So far so good, but going downwards doesn't convey the opposite by recouping energy – descending into a valley

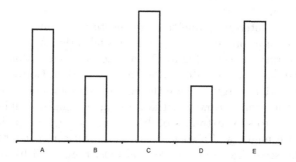

Fig. 2.1. Even without a scale drawn on the y-axis, we can easily perceive alternate bars to be about half the height of the remainder.

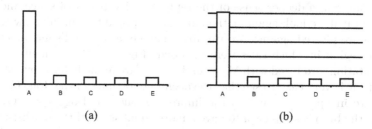

(a)   (b)

Fig. 2.2. If the bar heights are very different (a), we can use a device such as gridlines (b) to support our visual measuring skills.

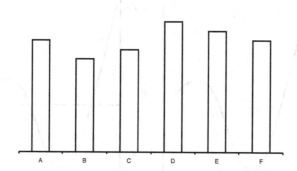

Fig. 2.3. B and D stand out fairly easily as being the lowest and highest values respectively, but it takes a moment to establish that C is the second to smallest, then A, F, and E. In fact, A and F are equal, but are probably too distant from each other for us to decide this with any certainty.

from my current position will cost nearly as much effort as then climbing back up to where I started.

This raises the interesting question of what to do about negative numbers and brings a realisation that, in scientific visualization at least, 'zero' is a somewhat arbitrary concept. Figure 2.4(a) shows a calculation of potential energy versus distance as two atoms approach each other. Convention equates the zero of potential energy – where the curve would level out – with infinite separation of the atoms. However, the framing rectangle, coupled with our natural tendency to spot extremes of data, leads the eye to the lowest point of the curve; we might well associate this point with a near-zero value if it weren't for the scale drawn on the vertical axis. Figure 2.4(b), on the other hand, reinforces the crossover simply by adding a horizontal line. Figure 2.5 demonstrates the equivalent effect for a surface view, where the addition of an axial system serves to confirm that the data fall below some notional but significant value.

We can gain a deeper sense of the representative power of space and the objects in it if we look again at the bar chart representation, but now where the data are plotted against two variables, namely a pet food's manufacturer and the region in which sales were recorded (Fig. 2.6). The benefits of this representation, produced with Microsoft® Excel, are immediately obvious. For example, it is very easy to see that the declining fortunes of the 'EasyChomp' brand are in opposite sense to the improving sales of 'DoggyGro'. Overall though, the brands seem each to have a more equal share of the market in the South East, compared with the South West and North. Interesting insights

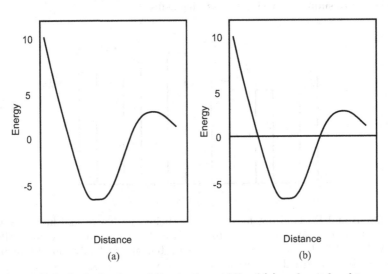

Fig. 2.4. The lack of a horizontal line in the middle of (a) makes it hard to perceive the curve as flowing above and below the zero value of energy that is, by contrast, perfectly evident in (b).

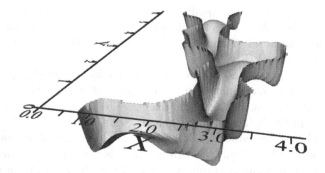

Fig. 2.5. Axes in the horizontal plane emphasise that the values of this surface lie below zero, in much the same way as the horizontal line in Fig. 2.4 helps to perceive some parts of that curve are above, and some below, zero. Image credit: IRIS Explorer, test data suite.

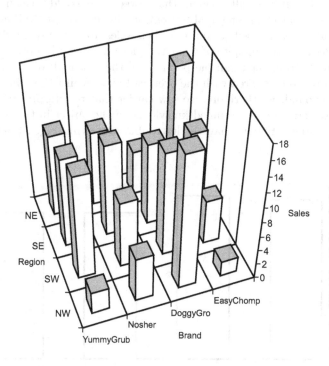

Fig. 2.6. Adding a third axis can allow more variables to be compared, but possibly at the expense of quantitative judgments.

indeed, but all are essentially qualitative in nature; we would not, from such a visualization, be able to detect that in the South East sales of 'Nosher' were ever-so slightly ahead of 'YummyGrub', even though this is easily seen once perspective is removed (Fig. 2.7).

Looking at Figs. 2.6 and 2.7 we can see that by introducing perspective into the drawing we have increased the insight that is available but reduced its value for making quantitative judgments. This is a trade-off that might be acceptable in the light of definite benefits, but as a general rule-of-thumb perspective should be avoided if it is unnecessary to the visualization and *must* be avoided if it will mislead. An example is the often-seen 'overdimension' effect used in business graphics. Figure 2.8(a) demonstrates a pie chart doing a perfectly good job of showing us that 'KleenCat' kitty litter and its competitor 'SweetNGo' have equal sales in percentage terms. The same chart (Fig. 2.8(b)) drawn as a cylinder (presumably to try to justify the unnecessary use of an elevated, as opposed to an overhead, view) gives us a very different impression. Here it is equally evident that 'SweetNGo' could take on the combined might of both 'NoPong' and 'KleenCat'. Executives at 'NiffLess' would also no doubt be surprised to find out their sales are actually nearly double those of 'PrittyKitty', in spite of what the picture seems to imply. The effect is quite simple to understand: pie portions in the east and west of the chart are foreshortened compared with the overhead view, whilst those in the north and south expand. Furthermore, we saw earlier that to interpret perspective correctly we rely on our presumed knowledge of the object in the scene. It is interesting to note that we have little trouble perceiving Fig. 2.9 as a quar-

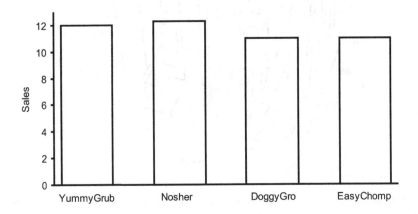

Fig. 2.7. The same information as appears in Fig. 2.6 for the South East allows a much more accurate assessment of the brands' relative sales, once perspective is removed.

tered disk, even though its (equal) segments have been subjected to the same distortion. However, the lack of prior expectations for the irregular object, combined with the distortion effect, causes our visual system to jump to the wrong conclusion and interpret the pieces as having incorrect sizes.

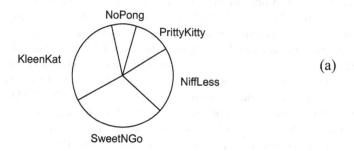

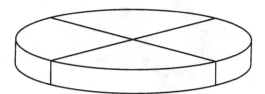

Fig. 2.8. Whilst an overhead view of a pie chart (a) gives an undistorted impression of the various brands' proportional share of the cat litter market, an elevated view (b) can give quite a different impression.

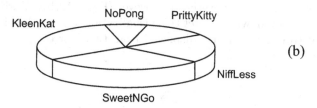

Fig. 2.9. When dealing with regular portions, however, we somehow manage to interpret even this elevated view correctly.

Such mistakes in a representation are obvious and easy to correct, but the next example shows that perspective can be a more insidious enemy. Figure 2.10 shows a surface view visualization of a mathematical function whose value, plotted as height above and below the plane, varies continuously according to position on the x- and y-axes (across and along the plane). As well as demonstrating the placement and relative sizes of its main features in the same way as a bar chart would, the form of this object gives us additional clues as to the data it represents. Shading gives the object apparent solidity and helps us to understand just how rapidly the data falls away into the trough. Highlights cue its curvature – clearly the peak of the function is not circular in cross-section. Such information is qualitative, though, and to obtain some quantitative insight we might use a contour plot as well (Fig. 2.11). A fairly common embellishment to a contour plot is to elevate each line according to the value it denotes. This can be advantageous if the software allows rotation of the object since our visual sense can partially reconstruct its underlying form (Fig. 2.12(a)), but at the same time we may derive some quantitative information by virtue of a colour key. Look what happens when we view this object from directly overhead, however (Fig. 2.12(b)). With all hints of a third axis removed, we interpret this visualization as a flat drawing, but whose peak and trough are clearly displaced from their correct positions shown in Fig. 2.11.

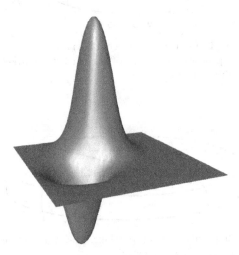

Fig. 2.10. The form of an object can give a good understanding of the speed of variation of the underlying data. Highlights show the curvature of a surface; here the narrowness of the reflection running towards the peak is a good clue that it is not circular in cross-section, an impression that would be confirmed as we move the object interactively. Image credit: IRIS Explorer, test data suite.

Fig. 2.11. Contours can give some feel for the underlying data and show its exact value, but only at certain points within the domain. Image credit: IRIS Explorer, test data suite.

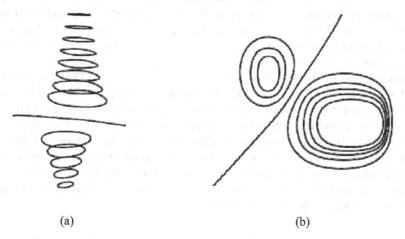

(a)   (b)

Fig. 2.12. Elevating contour lines into a type of surface (a) can give some qualitative insight and, if colour is used, include some quantitative capability. If such a visualization is viewed from overhead, however, we perceive it as a flat plane and the locations of the minimum and maximum appear shifted (b). Image credit: IRIS Explorer, test data suite.

2.1.2 Using Colour

Colour is an intrinsic part of most visualizations. Sometimes it is used to confirm an existing feature of a representation; for example, Fig. 2.10 in its original form was coloured from blue for the lowest values through magenta to red for the highest, reaffirming which is the peak and which is the trough of the object, even when the user rotates the image. The particular colour scheme – blue to red – is immediately suggestive of cold changing to hot, which is appropriate in this case because the variable being plotted is temperature. Had the colours chosen been yellow to green, say, then the user would have required a conscious effort to interpret their meanings. Colour can also give a way to add information about another variable without contributing to clutter in the image. For example, arrows representing the flow of air throughout a volume can be coloured to give an impression of the air's temperature too. This technique is common in meteorology and saves drawing more contours on the weather map than are absolutely necessary. Another example we will meet in Chap. 6 is called a height-field plot, where the heights above the plane indicate one variable and the colours another. This technique might be of use in geology, where heights could represent the terrain and colour the hardness of the constituent rock. If this information is presented as intersecting surfaces, however, the results are very difficult to interpret as each occludes the other at various points across the plane.

As with the usage of space, though, the use of colour sometimes requires caution. Apart from the obvious difficulty for certain individuals with anomalous colour vision (often – incorrectly – called 'colour blind'), there can be pitfalls even for those users whose colour vision is normal. For example, colours are affected by how an object is lit, appearing darker when in shade and washed out, or desaturated, where there are highlights. This can be serious if colour is being used to depict the value of a variable. The effect is more troublesome with a static visualization such as might appear in a book, but is less of a problem when the user can interact to rotate the object, since this moves the shading and highlights around, thereby helping to resolve any ambiguity. We also need to be aware that visual attention varies with the particular colour applied to an object together with its surroundings. The use, and possible abuse, of colour in visualization is sufficiently important to warrant a whole chapter later in this book.

2.1.3 Using Animation

Apart from three spatial dimensions, the only other dimension we meet in the real world is time. Though it is natural to express time as animation, there are choices to be made according to the goals of the visualization and, once again, the potential to mislead the user is there.

It is worthwhile to take a moment to clarify terms. In this book the term 'animation' is used to indicate movement caused by some procedure or program, rather than the user. Movement caused by the user is here termed 'interaction', but other authors may refer to this too as animation. Both types of movement depend on achieving good frame rates in the graphics – interaction accompanied by a jerky response from the object under scrutiny is nearly as disorientating as hearing your own speech played back to you a moment after you utter it. By means of a combination of the critical fusion frequency and our natural tendency to link static images together (beta movement), different pictures shown faster than about 20Hz will appear to blend into continuous, flicker-free motion. During interaction the geometry has therefore to re-render faster than this rate – limiting factors will include the number of polygons comprising the object and the sizes of any textures that have been applied. During animation the processing per frame also has to include the regeneration of the visualization for each new time step, or possibly re-reading a file of data to acquire the new time step. For large datasets or computationally intensive visualization techniques, therefore, 'live' animation might not be a possibility at all and we then have to resort to other means.

One such alternative is to 'tile' the display with the various frames. Figure 2.13 shows the development over six time steps of the function originally in Fig. 2.10. In fact, this visualization is simple enough to animate satisfac-

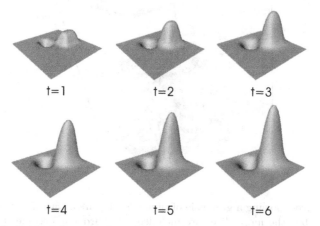

Fig. 2.13. Individual frames selected from an animation can give some impression of how a dataset varies over time and might also reveal details in the individual frames that would otherwise be missed. Image credit: IRIS Explorer, test data suite.

torily on even a modest workstation, though separating the frames like this gives an opportunity to look particularly at the form of the peak and trough as they develop during the simulation. Though not quite the analogue of the qualitative vs. quantitative insight that was discussed earlier, the effect is similar because looking at the animation gives an overall impression of the function's development, whilst looking at the frames shows small details that could otherwise have been missed. In an ideal world, therefore, we would aim to provide both mechanisms for a time-varying dataset.

The visualization in Fig. 2.13 is stationary, and yet it is providing information on data from the time dimension. If we now turn this idea on its head we can imagine a static dataset but whose visualization is animated. This is useful if the visualization technique can only cover part of the data at any one moment. Figure 2.14 shows a volume of data coming from a computed tomograph (CT) of a person's head. Although there is a technique that tries to show the whole such volume at once (see Chap. 6), it is computationally intensive for large datasets. Slices across the volume can give some impression of the overall variation of tissue density, but the conundrum is that the more we try to cover all the volume, the less we see because the intervening slices get in the way. One solution is to have a single slice but to pass it back and forth through the volume, so that our short-term visual memory can help reconstruct the whole picture. This should preferably be done with such fine changes in position that the slice looks to move smoothly, since if it 'jumps' then so too will our eyes in following it. Eye movement like this is called a saccade, and there is evidence that having a saccade occur between images

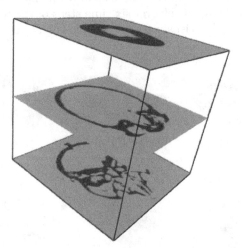

Fig. 2.14. Slices showing a greyscale of tissue density are a way of visualizing data in a volume, but the more slices are included, the harder it becomes to see their contents. Image credit: IRIS Explorer, test data suite.

is a good way of hiding changes in detail between them. Another difficulty in presenting information in this way is more mundane, namely misinterpreting the animation as having come from a time-varying, rather than a static, data set. This is easily addressed by labelling the display with an appropriate caption that counts up and down the positions of the slices as they are shown.

2.2 Misunderstanding Data

The previous section talked about how we can harness our perceptual skills to understand data, together with some of the risks that entails. Throughout though, there was an assumption that the basic representation was without fault. There is perhaps a more fundamental problem which we have to solve first, namely, how to correctly select and execute the visualization itself. The following two sections discuss this problem in general, but it is one we will return to throughout the rest of this book.

2.2.1 Using the Right Tool for the Right Job

This old workshop adage is not grammatically correct, but it serves as due warning for any visualization user who might imagine that it is sufficient just to put numbers into a drawing package and get a picture out. How many times on television and in newspapers do we see a line graph of average monthly share prices such as that in Fig. 2.15? A moment's thought shows this representation is absurd; if we follow the dotted vertical lines we can clearly read off

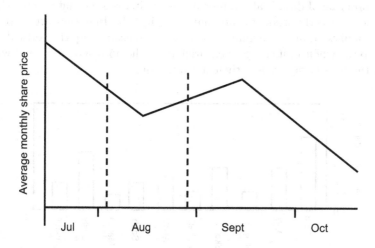

Fig. 2.15. The y-axis label indicates these are *average* monthly share prices, so how can it be possible to read off a value for the first week in August and another for the last week?

the share price for the last week in August and find it is different to the price in the first week in August, even though such variation *must* have already been subsumed into the average August price.

Knowing the application is important, because it is in the nature of data that some sets of points have no inherent order and for others their order is significant. Furthermore, some data varies continuously and some does not. Mixing up the different types when choosing which technique to use is one of the cardinal sins of visualization. Consider Fig. 2.16, which shows the sales of various manufacturers' cars at some distant year in the future. There is no sense in which we can think of an average between, say, Mercedes and Skoda, so to join up their data points and all the others' by using a line graph to represent the data would be nonsensical. This is *nominal* (or named) data, represented as a bar (some packages call it a column) chart. Being nominal data, we could shuffle the bars because this data has no inherent order, though we might choose to present them a particular way so as to make some special point. The share data in the paragraph above is subtly different – the average August price applies to the whole of August, which is why it is inappropriate to blend it with a little of July's price at the beginning of the month and a little of September's price towards the end. The strictly correct visualization of this type of data looks like the treads of a set of stairs or the tops of a battlement (Fig. 2.17), though often a bar chart has to suffice. If we were to use a bar chart though, we couldn't expect to shuffle the bars, like we could with the cars, and still understand what is going on. This is because September follows August just as surely as thunder follows lightning. In short, this data is *ordinal* (its order is important) but is discontinuous (doesn't join on) from one month to the next.

The ordering of data is also important when items are counted into 'bins', or ranges, such as the student exam marks in Fig. 2.18. Here they are correctly shown as a histogram – by definition, each count measured up the vertical axis applies to the whole of its range measured along the horizontal axis, and when plotted the bins always reflect their natural sequence.

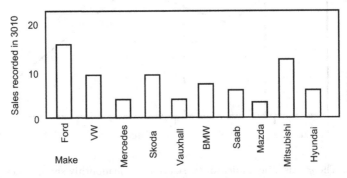

Fig. 2.16. Nominal, or named, data requires a bar or column chart for visualization. Bars can be shuffled but still convey their original meaning.

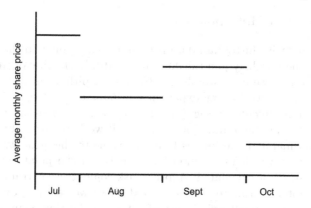

Fig. 2.17. The share data of Fig. 2.15 was in reality ordinal but discontinuous, meaning that the average price for any one month might be very different to its neighbours, but prices should nonetheless be plotted in order.

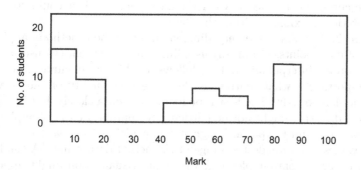

Fig. 2.18. Counts of items in various 'bins' or ranges can be shown using a histogram, where the count measured up the y-axis applies to the whole of its designated range along the x-axis.

2.2.2 The Perils of Interpolation

A common error with histogram data is to assign each count to the midpoint of its bin and then blithely join the dots (Fig. 2.19). In the case of the student marks data we find we have stumbled into another pitfall, since students are often negative but never, in my experience, in number.

Of course, our difficulty in Fig. 2.19 started when we chose the wrong type of representation for the data. However, even if we have correctly identified the data as ordinal and continuous from one value to the next, we still have to take care how we fill in, or interpolate, between the points at which it has been measured or calculated. Another risk comes if we extrapolate data, that is, attempt to estimate values beyond those we really know for sure. Figure 2.20 shows a hypothetical case of a test combustion chamber that is being monitored at regular intervals for the concentration of a particular gas. The concentration of gas in the chamber cannot drop below zero nor, since the chamber is sealed, can it rise above a certain amount. Here, then, are two risk points in the visualization: if the curve used to join the known data values is too free-flowing, then it might imply there are negative concentrations at A; if the curve is continued beyond the data points at B it could rise above the theoretical maximum within the chamber.

Figure 2.21 shows three very different interpolation methods applied to one set of data points. Graph (a) uses linear interpolation, (b) uses a piece-wise monotonic interpolant, and (c) follows a cubic Bessel curve. The names are unimportant – what matters is the increasing fluidity of the curves in going from left to right. The first type follows the data closely, but its sudden changes of direction might not be particularly appropriate to the application. In contrast the third type, although it has a pleasing appearance, exhibits plotted values well outside the range of the actual data values. A similar effect can occur in contour plotting, where the visualization might appear to have peaks and troughs that are respectively higher and lower than known maxima and minima in the data. In between these two is a curve that preserves the local maxima and minima of the original data but with less marked changes of gradient at the data points. The choice as to which to use is not just an aesthetic one, since visualization may be used to support some key decision. For example, if these were predicted pest numbers and our goal was to decide whether and when to spray with insecticide, then we might make very different decisions purely on the basis of the method used to plot the curve – clearly an undesirable state of affairs.

We might well ask which of the curves in Fig. 2.21 is correct, to which the answer is both "all of them" and "none of them"! That is, they all qualify as valid interpolants because they all pass through each data point as required, but on the other hand each has been applied arbitrarily without knowing if it is appropriate. Rather than thinking of this as visualizing the data, we need to think of the problem as attempting to reconstruct what is *underlying* the data, further evidence that it is just as important to know the application as it is to

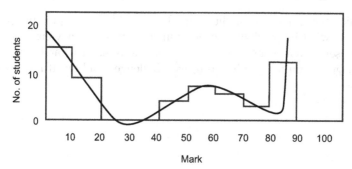

Fig. 2.19. Another nonsensical representation, this time obtained by trying to show histogram data as a line graph.

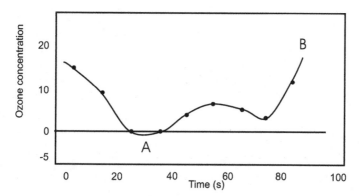

Fig. 2.20. Interpolation (such as at point A) and extrapolation (point B) both present risks in visualization. Here, poor control of interpolation gives us a negative concentration of gas, which is physically impossible. Extrapolation might likewise imply there is more ozone than can ever be generated by this system.

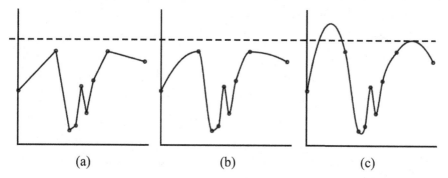

(a) (b) (c)

Fig. 2.21. Suppose the horizontal dotted line shows the pest concentrations that usually trigger spraying. We can see that the three very different interpolants would lead to different decisions, even though the actual data is the same in each case. Image credit: IRIS Explorer, test data suite.

know which techniques we might apply. Regrettably, many plotting packages do not state what interpolant or other numerical method they employ, leaving it to the user to make the right decision on the basis of what he or she sees in the image. If you feel you're up to the challenge, read on. If not, close this book now!

Problems

2.1. Look in a newspaper or magazine for graphical representations of every-day quantities. Can you identify one example each of nominal and ordinal data? If the data is of ordinal type, does the quantity that is plotted vary continuously, is it discontinuous, or is it defined across some range of the or-dinal data? Can you find any examples where the representation chosen gives the wrong impression of the data used to generate it?

2.2. Pick up some everyday objects and turn them in the light. What type of surface do they have (is it matte or shiny, for example), and what does this tell you about their shape? Are your visual observations confirmed by touching the object?

3

Models and Software

When any new discipline starts out, the initial rush to chart the unknown is usually followed by a period of reflection and harmonisation. A common product of this phase is a model or models that try to place some order on the topic. Visualization was no different; in fact, rather more models of visualization were probably produced than for most disciplines.

Models are important because they provide a framework for thinking through ideas. They allow comparisons to be made of different approaches – in this chapter they will serve as a basis for describing different visualization scenarios, and for thinking about some common approaches to constructing software.

3.1 A Dataflow Model of Visualization

As the NSF report mentioned in Chap. 1 stated very clearly, visualization is intrinsically bound up with scientific analysis, which in turn affords a cyclical description. The stages to be considered typically begin with mathematical modelling of the natural phenomenon being studied. Simplifications might then be made that allow a simulation to be programmed in the computer and some numerical results generated. These results are next analysed with the help of visualization. Depending on the outcome of the analysis, previous stages of the process may be revisited. For example, the visualization might suggest that the numerical results are not sufficiently accurate, so the simulation is re-run with different tolerances. These new results might, however, show up a more fundamental problem in the mathematical description, necessitating remodelling followed by reprogramming. The cycle continues either until a satisfactory explanation of the phenomenon can be found or until the current approach can be discounted as not creditable.

Breaking down the overall endeavour in this way led to a more detailed analysis of what constitutes visualization, and ultimately to the two dataflow models that are mostly referred to today. These models recognise that visualization as a whole is composed of a pipeline of transformations that gradually turns raw data into a pictorial representation. Any visualization process can therefore be written as a directed acyclic graph (Fig. 3.1); changing a variable at any stage in the pipeline causes only this and its dependent stages to recompute, with obvious benefits in terms of efficiency.

Two broad themes are discernible in these two models' descriptions: one deals with the transformations involved and the other with the data each generates. Thus the first gives us three separate stages of data filtering (or data enrichment), mapping and rendering, whilst the second furnishes the derived data, abstract visualization object (AVO), and displayable image that these produce. Figure 3.2 puts the two themes together into one diagram.

The process begins with raw data entering the filtering stage. In common parlance 'filtering' usually means selective removal, but here the term is used in its more general, engineering sense, namely to transform data from one form into another. The alternative term 'data enrichment' makes this wider meaning explicit. Probably the commonest enrichment, especially for raw data coming from a simulation, is to interpolate between data points at which values have been calculated. As Sect. 2.2.2 showed, this has to be done with some care and due regard for the phenomenon being modelled. If data come from experimental measurements and are noisy, they could need smoothing before being visualized. Figure 3.3 shows how interference can generate an electrical signal that fluctuates widely, masking an overall response that, by contrast, rises gradually and then falls away. Finally, there may be filtering to produce a lesser quantity of raw data that is otherwise unchanged from the original. Figure 3.4 shows a CT scan subsampled to one-quarter of its original density and then reinstated to include all the data. Although visually similar to a smoothing operation, subsampling is fundamentally different because data are ignored, not folded in with their neighbours to make new values.

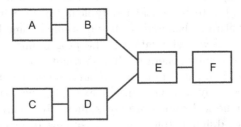

Fig. 3.1. A directed acyclic graph of processes can represent efficiency gains compared with an application that incorporates all its transformations into one, monolithic structure. In a dataflow application, a change at B will cause E and F to recompute but not A, C, or D.

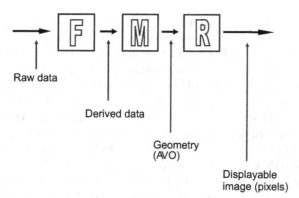

Raw data

Derived data

Geometry
(AVO)

Displayable
image (pixels)

Fig. 3.2. A model of visualization that incorporates the processes of filtering, mapping, and rendering in order to transform raw data into derived data, then geometry in the form of an abstract visualization object, and finally the pixels needed to make a displayable image.

Fig. 3.3. Smoothing experimentally measured data (solid line) may reveal an underlying trend (dotted) not evident in the individual values themselves.

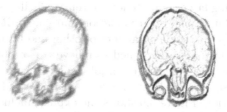

Fig. 3.4. Subsampling data can make a large dataset easier to manipulate in the early stages of investigation, reinstating all of the data in order for final conclusions to be drawn. Image credit: IRIS Explorer, test data suite.

After filtering to produce derived data comes the mapping stage to produce an AVO. An AVO is an imaginary object with attributes such as size, colour, transparency, texture, and so on. Data is mapped to these attributes in order to represent it visually. Thus temperature might control the colour of the object, ranging from blue for cold through to red for hot; sales of cars might determine the length of bars in a chart. The particular object into whose attributes data are mapped depends on the visualization technique that is chosen, which in turn depends on the type of data being investigated. How to classify data in order to choose a suitable technique is the topic of Chap. 5. In general, though, there is no one-to-one mapping of technique to data, nor of data to attributes, so the experimentation that occurs is this stage is a defining characteristic that sets visualization apart from data presentation.

The final stage is to render the AVO into a displayable image. Here the object might need to be rotated, translated or scaled; it could be viewed with perspective or have other depth cues applied. As Sect. 2.1.1 described, the form of the object can give clues about the data it represents, so the application of lighting is another important aspect of the rendering process.

3.2 Visualization Scenarios

The dataflow model has been very useful in describing extensions to the original paradigm; amongst them are computational steering, distributed visualization, and collaborative visualization.

3.2.1 Computational Steering

One of the stated aims of visualization in the NSF report was to enable the steering of simulations. Until that time, scientists had carried out their investigations by submitting large compute jobs to remote facilities and viewing their output some time later, once the calculation had ended. Regrettably, a quite common finding was that some parameter or other had been mis-specified and the output was useless. Steering aimed to relieve this problem; by seeing the output whilst it was being generated, a job could be halted if going awry, or even have its course corrected by changing a parameter between individual steps of the simulation. Figure 3.5 shows the explicit inclusion of a 'simulate' process into the filter-map-render pipeline. Thus the input to the filter stage is still raw data but now it is being produced on-line for immediate visualization. The simplicity of this diagram belies the difficulty of making this idea work; programs constructed originally for a 'numbers in, numbers out' approach sometimes need a complete overhaul of their architecture in order to be steered. There is also the problem of how to record the progress of the scientist's interactions, since sometimes the best solution is not immediately evident, requiring a roll-back of the experimentation.

A number of attempts at computational steering were made soon after the publication of the NSF report but it has recently experienced a revival of interest – Chap. 8 contains further details.

3.2.2 Distributed and Collaborative Visualization

A knowledge of what is flowing between each stage of the dataflow pipeline provides a convenient means to describe distributed visualization. Early attempts at client-server visualization tended to serve pictures, in other words, virtually the whole of the pipeline was running on the server and the local machine had only to display the pixels, sent in some standard image format (Fig. 3.6(a)). As web browsers became available that could handle the virtual reality modelling language (VRML), it proved possible to move the client-server dividing line further back (Fig. 3.6(b)). VRML allowed the communication of three-dimensional data and gave the client the flexibility to render and interact with the object as they pleased, rather than simply looking at a static image.

Fig. 3.5. A model of visualization that incorporates the simulation process, as well as filtering, mapping, and rendering. The simulation's output is visualized as it is produced, so that the computation can be halted or changed according to what is seen in the results.

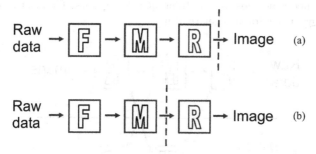

Fig. 3.6. A model describing client-server visualization. In (a), virtually all of the pipeline runs on the server that is left of the dashed line and the local software need only display images. In (b), geometry in the form of VRML or its successor X3D is served, and the user of the client software can choose their own rendering operations to apply locally, rather than have these dictated by the server.

Closely bound up with distributed visualization is collaborative visualization, where two or more geographically distributed users work together on a shared problem. Depending on which aspects they share and which they keep separate, more or less of the pipeline might need to be distributed. For example, a case where one worker controls all of the data and processes whilst the other just looks at the images will seem to the second user very like the pipeline in Fig. 3.6(a). At the opposite end of the spectrum we could imagine sharing at the application level, with each person's display, mouse movements, and button presses being transmitted to the other. Figure 3.7 shows a scenario somewhere in between these two. As in the diagrams of distributed visualization, the dotted line indicates the boundary between two networked machines, this time allocated one per user. In this instance the raw data remains private to the user of the upper pipeline, whilst the derived data (the output of the filter stage) is shared with their colleague, operating the lower one. The two workers use different mapping and render processes (the lower pipeline has primes to indicate this) but they share their AVOs. The overall result is that each user has a different image but of the same geometry.

Just as in computational steering, these architecture diagrams hide some complex implementation details. In distributed visualization the challenge on the server side is to develop parametrised, batch versions of software that was originally intended for interactive use. Communication between server and client is also an issue, since it involves transmission, via an external medium, of data that would normally remain confined within a single visualization program. In collaborative visualization there are likewise decisions to be made concerning the transmission of data: should this be transferred from peer-to-peer or via a central server; are late-comers to the collaboration to be sent the shared elements automatically or only with the consent of their peers? There is also the issue of overall control: is there to be a concept of one user 'taking the floor' during the interaction, during which time the others must watch passively; if there is no floor protocol, how will the system deal with simultaneous actions by the different participants? Chapter 8 once again contains suggestions for further reading.

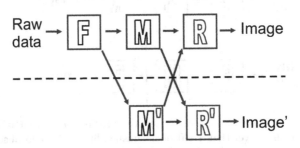

Fig. 3.7. In collaborative visualization two or more users can work on a shared problem. Here they are each looking at the same derived data, but using their own preferred visualization technique and sharing its output.

3.3 Visualization Software

The dataflow model described above can be used to describe any software that transforms data into a visual representation, but it has also been used in the interface design of a particular type of visualization toolkit known as application-builder software, or modular visualization environment (MVE). This section first charts the driving influences in the development of this and other types of visualization software and then goes on to discuss some present-day examples.

3.3.1 Historical Context

In MVEs, filter, map, and render facilities are provided as a set of modules that the user connects together in a workspace, using visual programming, or drag-and-drop editing. As data passes through each module it is transformed in some way and flows to the next in the pipeline. The final module the transformed data encounters is a render process that displays it.

A number of systems using this visual programming paradigm first appeared in the late 1980s and early 1990s: apE, originally an abbreviation of 'animation production Environment', developed by the Ohio Supercomputer Graphics Project (OSGP) at the University of Ohio; the Advanced Visualization System (AVS) originally developed by Stellar Computer; IBM Visualization Data Explorer; IRIS Explorer originally a product of Silicon Graphics, Inc (SGI); Khoros from Khoral Research, Inc, University of New Mexico.

Coincidentally, the first two in this alphabetical list are recognised as the forerunners of this genre, though all five were established players by the mid-1990s. MVEs were not the first software systems on the visualization scene, however, but an innovation that tried to balance the ease-of-use of 'turnkey' visualizers with the flexibility provided by traditional programming approaches. Turnkey visualizers aimed to provide an appropriate visualization with little or no prior learning or customisation, but could be restrictive in their capabilities. Programmed solutions, on the other hand, gave ultimate flexibility but at the cost of software development. By adding modules to an MVE the system's functionality could be extended beyond that originally envisaged, providing some flexibility; visual programming required users to construct their own applications but without the need for low-level coding, providing some ease-of-use. Flexibility and ease-of-use were thus seen as two largely opposing scales, with turnkey approaches and traditional programming at opposite ends of the spectrum and visual programming somewhere in the middle (Fig. 3.8).

3.3.2 Current Approaches

In the early days of visualization software Fig. 3.8 gave a fairly accurate description of individual offerings; nowadays, however, a single product rarely occupies just one position in the spectrum. Software developers realise that for their package to appeal widely they must strive to include features that will give the best of all worlds in terms of its flexibility and ease-of-use.

A discussion of some currently available software will serve to illustrate, but the same analysis can be applied to any of the many software packages on the market or available to download for free. For example, Tecplot from Tecplot, Inc presents users with a mouse-operated Workspace in which it is very easy to select 2D, 3D, and animated visualizations of data. The same Workspace can, however, be extended to include new functionality written in a language such as C++. This new functionality, termed an 'add-on', integrates seamlessly as if part of the standard software, giving a tool that is flexible from a developer's point of view but remains easy for the client to use. The Interactive Data Language (IDL) from Research Systems, Inc is a command language with an extensive and extensible library of data access, numerical and visualization routines. This fulfills the requirement for flexibility, whilst the "iTools", a set of pre-built interactive utilities, provide ease-of-use that is more typical of a turnkey visualizer. PV-WAVE from Visual Numerics, Inc is also a command language with considerable power and hence flexibility, though many of its users will know it via its Navigator interface, which gives ease-of-use via its interactive point-and-click visualizations. For those wanting to program in a general-purpose language, the Visualization Toolkit (VTK) from Kitware, Inc is a C++ class library. This powerful resource is therefore available to anyone with a knowledge of C++ and, by means of language bindings, to programmers in Java, the Tool Command Language (Tcl), or Python. Ease-of-use for non-programmers is catered for by the Parallel Visualization Application (ParaView), a large-data turnkey visualizer built on top of VTK which can therefore draw on its functionality. As can be seen from this analy-

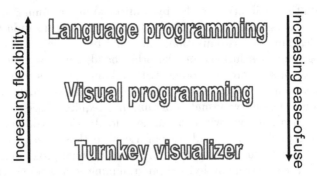

Fig. 3.8. A visualization solution programmed for a specific purpose (top) could be made to fulfill virtually any requirement but at the expense of writing, testing, and debugging it. In contrast, turnkey visualizers (bottom) were written with general requirements in mind for a variety of subsequent uses and therefore might not suit everyone's needs precisely. Application builders (centre) tried to simplify the construction of a range of solutions by means of their visual programming interfaces.

sis most visualization software, though it may have a primary locator on the spectrum, will also include characteristics from either side and, sometimes, from the furthest extremes of the scale.

The gap targetted by the original MVEs may therefore have closed somewhat, but that has not rendered the principle or its products redundant; visual programming remains a popular paradigm. Systems using this approach have continued to appear including, amongst others: Amira from Mercury Computer Systems, Inc; the COllaborative VIsualization and Simulation Environment (COVISE) from Visual Engineering Solutions (VISENSO) GmbH.; SCIRun (pronounced "ski-run") from the Scientific Computing and Imaging (SCI) Institute at the University of Utah; and Yet-another-COVISE (YAC) from the High Performance Computing Center, Stuttgart (HLRS).

Of the five original dataflow MVEs one, apE, has fallen by the wayside but four are in continuing development: the Advanced Visualization System (as AVS/Express) is now a product of Advanced Visual Systems; IBM Visualization Data Explorer has become the Open Visualization Data Explorer (OpenDX); IRIS Explorer is now developed and marketed by the Numerical Algorithms Group (NAG) Ltd; Khoros has become the VisiQuest system from AccuSoft Corporation. Refinements variously made to these systems since their first appearance include: data referencing to replace the copying of data from one process to another; coercion of several modules' functionality into a single process; the inclusion of loop and control constructs allowing more powerful programs to be constructed; customisation of the system's appearance without recourse to low-level programming; and, hiding the evidence of visual programming behind an interface that looks more like a turnkey.

Choosing between software today is therefore not so much an issue of deciding whether a product is a turnkey, is an application builder, or uses a programming language and library, but determining where its emphasis lies and how this fits with requirements. Three key questions to ask are, is the exposure (such as occurs in visual programming) of the underlying framework of benefit to the application and its users; does the software provide the necessary techniques and, if it doesn't or these are not yet known, is it extensible; and, most importantly of all, is it likely to be usable by the target audience? Easy questions – not always easy answers.

Problems

3.1. Type "visualization software" into an Internet search engine and choose one of the many pages that describe a commercially available or open source software product. To what extent does your chosen subject look like a turnkey, application builder, or programming language and library? Does it have features from different parts of the spectrum, or are there complementary products that use it and extend its classification? If the product is commercial, are all the features available for a single payment or must they be purchased separately?

You may have to search ancillary information such as case studies and documentation in order to answer fully. Make notes as you go along to assist in summarising your research.

3.2. Think about a potential client with a visualization problem, such as your employer or lecturer. Would the person you have chosen require some general-purpose package or software tailored to a particular need? Would he require easy-to-use software or could he master traditional or visual programming? The answers to these two questions sometimes reveal conflicting requirements: if your client requires tailored but easy-to-use software, is anyone available to do the customisation or would this incur additional purchase costs, for example for consultancy charges?

Now think about several clients such as your office colleagues or the staff on your course. Does this change the type of software you would procure?

4

Colour in Scientific Visualization

Unlike the qualitative use of colour in computer graphics, where the aim is generally to add realism to a scene, in scientific visualization colour is more likely to convey quantitative information. Colour thus acts as an additional degree of freedom, usually used when the three spatial dimensions that we can readily perceive have already been allocated to data. This special requirement to represent numerical data makes it necessary to understand what constitutes colour and how it is perceived, and to have an idea of its potential and limitations.

4.1 The Electromagnetic Spectrum

Most books covering colour begin with a diagram of the electromagnetic spectrum – the relatively small portion occupied by visible radiation (light) is indeed noteworthy, as is the realisation that such diverse phenomena as X-rays, light, and radio are all comprised of the same coupled electric and magnetic fields, only with very different wavelengths. Figure 4.1 plots the key players, from gamma rays to medium/longwave radio. As far as is possible within the accuracy of the drawing, the vertical distance occupied by the thick black line corresponds to the actual wavelengths of light that we perceive as violet (at shorter wavelengths) through to red (longer wavelengths).

It is surprising, then, that our rich perception of the world around us can come from such a tiny piece of the scale. Even more so is the realisation that the scale itself is logarithmic, that is, equal distances are assigned not to the numbers, but to the power of the numbers, in this case with a base of ten. Thus $10^3 = 1000$ is the same distance along the axis from 10^2 (100) as 100 is from 10. This makes the differences in wavelengths truly staggering. Waves of visible light, at just 100s of nanometres long (1 nm $= 10^{-9}$m), are small enough to pack about 2 million into every metre, whereas the ones that bring in the breakfast show each morning are the same order of size as the room you eat breakfast in.

4.2 Colour Perception

Colour vision is not a capability possessed of all sighted creatures, many of which are only sensitive to the intensity of incoming light. Perception of colour is based additionally on a sensitivity to the *frequency* of the light, which is inversely proportional to its wavelength. The problem for early researchers was to propose a mechanism that could allow us to see many different colours but without requiring there to be an equivalent number of different receptors, each 'tuned' to some particular colour. The now-accepted theory, termed the tristimulus theory, is that there are just three types of colour receptor, each of which is stimulated preferentially by long-, medium- or short-wavelength light. When light of a particular wavelength falls on the retina, the different receptors, or cone cells, respond in differing degrees. Their combined signals are interpreted as a sensation of a single colour. Although these different receptors in fact each respond over a range of wavelengths they are often for convenience given the names 'red', 'green' and 'blue' cones.

Figure 4.2 shows the peak cone sensitivities of an individual with normal colour vision, relative to the full range of colours. The most common forms of anomalous colour vision concern the red and green (bottom and middle) cones, rather than the blue (top). For someone with a deficiency in the red system, one explanation is that this response curve is shifted up towards the green.

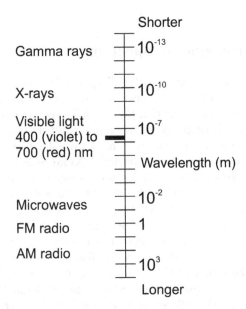

Fig. 4.1. The electromagnetic spectrum covers radiation as apparently diverse as gamma rays, light, and radio waves, but in fact these comprise the same coupled, oscillating electric and magnetic fields. 1 nm $= 10^{-9}$m. Data sources: Open University Science Data Book and the BBC web site.

For someone with a corresponding deficiency in the green system, the peak of the green curve is presumably shifted down towards the longer wavelengths. Since in either case the normal separation of the response curves is reduced, both types of anomaly result in a reduced range of colours being distinguished in the part of the spectrum normally seen as red blending through orange and yellow to green. The actual degree to which colours appear similar depends on the extent of the anomaly – some people are unaware they have any deficiency until subjected to a specialised colour perception test. The third type of colour deficiency involves the blue cones but is much less common than the other two.

True colour blindness, that is, where someone has no functioning cone cells and therefore cannot distinguish any colours, is extremely rare. Referring to someone with anomalous colour vision as 'colour blind' thus doesn't tell the whole story, since some range of colours is seen. This will be a restricted range, though, and the consequences of this for scientific visualization will be touched on later. It is also not particularly illuminating to ask *how* a particular colour is seen by someone with a colour vision deficiency, for example, whether red appears as beige or orange. Whilst these are different colours to someone with normal colour perception, to someone without it they might just be different labels apparently arbitrarily applied to the same thing. Ultimately we can never determine what anyone, anomalous or not, experiences from any particular colour. We all, including people with colour anomaly, know that grass is green only because we are told so when young, and we come to associate

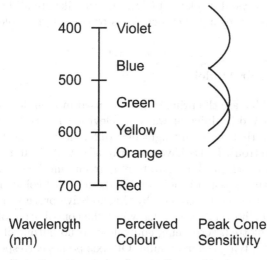

Wavelength (nm)   Perceived Colour   Peak Cone Sensitivity

Fig. 4.2. Cone cells in the retina are preferentially sensitive to certain wavelengths of visible light but respond across a wide range. Thus most colours, with the exception of blue and red at the extreme ends of the spectrum, are sensed by a mixture of responses. Note that, in contrast with Fig. 4.1, this plot follows a linear rather than a logarithmic scale.

the sensation of looking at grass with the colour we subsequently call 'green'. When we then look at another object that evokes the same sensation we give it the label 'green', too. Colours that evoke that same 'green' sensation for someone with colour anomaly might, however, look different to someone with normal colour vision and thus usually be given a different colour label. This distinctiveness, or lack of it, of different colours is the principle behind the colour plate tests that appear to show a number to a subject with normal colour vision and no number, or a different number, to someone with a deficiency.

4.3 Modelling Colour

The problem of how to produce colours for computer graphics is in some ways the converse of that presented to early researchers proposing a theory of colour vision. Whereas in colour vision there was a need to understand how so many colours can be seen without having equally many receptors, in output device engineering we have to give the appearance of many colours but without having light emitters tuned to every required frequency. Of course, the tristimulus theory comes to our aid here, because if we can sense many colours with three receptors, it follows that adding together three primary colours of light should do a fair job of simulating the many in between. This was Thomas Young's discovery and is the principle on which televisions, data projectors, liquid crystal displays (LCD), and the like are all based, emitting light at just three wavelengths chosen so as to cover the visible spectrum as best we can.

4.3.1 RGB Colour Model

Red, green, and blue are the primary colours used in such devices. Physically this may be achieved in different ways: a television has three types of phosphor in its screen that each emit light of a different wavelength when struck by a beam of electrons; LCDs have an array of coloured filters that give the light coming from each pixel a separate red, green, and blue component. Regardless of how the emission is accomplished, the RGB colour model applies to any device that generates colours by this additive process (Fig. 4.3). This model has three orthogonal axes along which the contribution of the different components are plotted, zero being equivalent to no output of that primary and 1 (or 255) signifying the maximum. Off-axis points correspond to colours that are seen by mixture, thus for example $(1, 1, 0)$ corresponds to yellow and $(0, 1, 1)$ to cyan. White $(= (1, 1, 1))$ and black $(= (0, 0, 0))$ are at opposite corners of the resulting cube, connected by a line of greys. Complementary colours, i.e. those which sum to white, can be found by reflecting any point on the cube through its centre.

The colour model is an abstract description; it cannot, for example, say precisely what $(1, 1, 0)$ will look like, because it makes no reference to the particular wavelengths of the primaries used. Moreover these wavelengths need not (and typically do not) match the peak cone sensitivities seen in Fig. 4.2 and where standards *have* been defined for certain devices, these may have changed over time. As Thomas Young discovered, the choice of wavelengths is quite wide provided there is reasonable separation. Different choices of primaries do, however, affect the proportion of all the visible colour combinations that can be reproduced by the particular device. The subset of colours that can be produced by any one device is termed its colour gamut.

4.3.2 HSV Colour Model

RGB is a useful model when describing how colours are produced by a computer monitor – roughly speaking, turning up the voltage on the electron gun assigned to, say, the red phosphor moves the colour's coordinate in the cube parallel to x and in a positive sense, whereas turning it down translates the point in the opposite direction. It is less useful for defining a colour intuitively: how many people would be able to quote the RGB values that would make

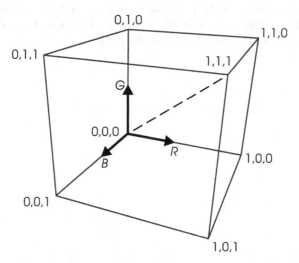

Fig. 4.3. The RGB colour model plots the contribution of each primary along the corresponding axes, which together form three edges of a cube. Red, green, and blue are respectively denoted $(1, 0, 0)$, $(0, 1, 0)$, and $(0, 0, 1)$; their complementary colours cyan, magenta, and yellow are the mixture colours $(0, 1, 1)$, $(1, 0, 1)$, and $(1, 1, 0)$ found on the opposite vertices. Black, at the origin of the cube $(= (0, 0, 0))$ and white $(= (1, 1, 1))$ are joined by a body diagonal (shown dotted) comprising shades of grey. Points along this line all have $R = G = B$.

their monitor emit coral pink?[1] If we think of RGB as useful for engineering the production of colours, then what is needed is a corresponding model that can describe them conveniently.

Perceptually we can think of a colour in terms of its named hue, such as yellow or green, and then additionally how pure a tint or how dark a shade it is. Figure 4.4 shows the inverted-cone colour model based on hue, saturation, and value, that allows just such a description. Hues vary according to the angle of rotation around the cone's axis, whilst saturation denotes how pure a colour is. Saturation is least along the central axis and greatest (purest) on the sides of the cone. 'Value' describes how dark a colour is and is least (darkest) at the point of the cone and greatest on its (upward-facing) circular base. The cone can thus be visualised as a circular disk of full-value colours sitting atop a sequence of progressively smaller and darker ones, culminating in a black point at the tip. This is how the model is often presented in computer graphics applications, namely as a colour wheel corresponding to the top of Fig. 4.4 together with a slider to vary the vertical coordinate.

Like RGB, the HSV model is additive; indeed, the two models are linked mathematically such that any colour specified in one can be transformed into a description in terms of the axes of the other. We can see the basis of this link by standing the RGB model on its black vertex and looking down. In this orientation the colours on the hue disk correspond to the hexagon of colours outlined by the vertices of the RGB cube (Fig. 4.5), whilst the line of greys in the cube matches the central axis of the HSV cone.

---

[1] I do in fact know someone who can do this, but he freely admits he has been working too long in computer graphics.

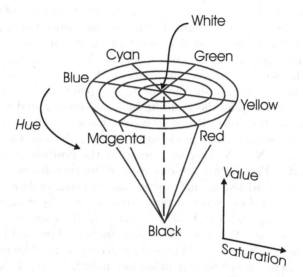

Fig. 4.4. The HSV colour model consists of a disk of colours that are fully saturated on the rim and become gradually less pure towards the centre, which is white. The concentric rings thus show the positions of colours of different hue but the same saturation. Colours become gradually darker (decrease in value) as the black point is approached. As in Fig. 4.3, the dotted line comprises shades of grey.

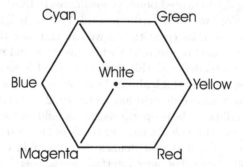

Fig. 4.5. Looking directly down the line of greys in the RGB cube reveals a hexagon whose vertices correspond to the colours seen around the HSV colour disk.

4.3.3 Relating RGB and HSV

Figure 4.6 demonstrates graphically the conversion between these two models. In (a), the arrows depict the axes of the RGB cube, within which two square-shaped surfaces have been plotted. The one on the back faces of the cube is for saturation set at its maximum, 1, and the one projecting into the body of the cube is for value set at 0.5. Since all points on these two surfaces respectively have $S = 1$ and $V = 0.5$, it follows that, on the line where they intersect, each colour there must also have both $S = 1$ and $V = 0.5$. Choosing a particular hue narrows down the line to one point, i.e., one colour. Hue starts at the line drawn on the value surface and sweeps round anticlockwise in the direction of the arrow. Red is by convention at $H = 0$, so the indicated point's coordinates in the HSV model are $(0, 1, 0.5)$, which we would call dark red (Fig. 4.6(b)). Now, looking once more at the position of the point in the RGB model (Fig. 4.6(a)), we can read off its coordinates as $(0.5, 0, 0)$, which corresponds to red at half power and no green or blue component. Decomposing this colour into two parts gives a clue why it corresponds to dark red, since $(1, 0, 0)/2 + (0, 0, 0)/2 = (0.5, 0, 0)$, the colour we are looking for. This equation says that if we mix equal amounts of red and black we get dark red, which is what we would expect intuitively. It must be remembered, though, that here we are mixing lights not paints, so 'black light' is just synonymous with 'no light'.

The remainder of Fig. 4.6 shows the derivation of pale green. Green, at $H = 0.33$, is one-third of full-circle distant from red at $H = 0$ so its coordinates in the HSV model (d) are $(0.33, 0.5, 1)$. In (c), the cone-shaped surface of saturation is for $S = 0.5$ and the three-sided surface shows 'value' at its maximum, 1, so reading the indicated point's coordinates in RGB gives $(0.5, 1, 0.5)$. Decomposing as before we get $(0, 1, 0)/2 + (1, 1, 1)/2 = (0.5, 1, 0.5)$, the colour we are looking for. From its constituents we can thus say that pale green is made from equal amounts of green and white, as we would expect.

So, with no pun intended, can this method be used in reverse to shed light on coral pink? First we must think about the colour itself – pale reddish-orange is perhaps the closest simple description – $(1, 0, 0)/2 + (1, 1, 0)/4 + (1, 1, 1)/4$ combines red and yellow in the proportions 2:1 and adds some white. Given the approximate nature of this calculation, our result of $(1, 0.5, 0.25)$ is remarkably close to the value $(1, 0.5, 0.3)$ that defines this colour in computer drawing and graphics applications. For user interface work, therefore, it is common to find that colours can be specified intuitively using their hue, saturation, and value, with the program then performing the conversion to RGB so that the device can output the required amounts of the three primary colours. In scientific visualization, however, mapping colours to data is done using whichever model yields the simplest description – some examples in the next section will illustrate.

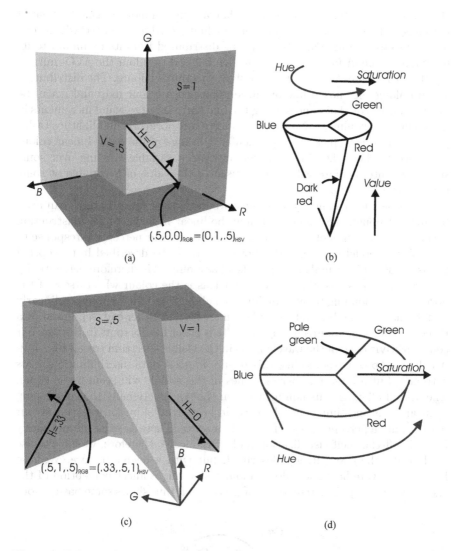

Fig. 4.6. Relating the RGB and HSV colour models. (a) and (b) show the derivation of dark red; (c) and (d) show the derivation of pale green. A surface of constant value always has a square shape but grows larger and moves further from the RGB origin as value increases. This surface is shown carrying lines along which hue is constant – these lines circulate anticlockwise with increasing hue when looking towards the RGB origin. A surface of constant saturation is a six-sided cone that grows wider as S increases. At S=1, adjacent pairs of sides become co-planar and the cone assumes a square shape reminiscent of the value surface. In all cases the point of the cone is located at the RGB origin.

4.4 Mapping Data to Colours

Having looked at two colour models that are in common usage, the task of mapping data to colours becomes one of finding a line or curve within one of these shapes along which data can be distributed from its minimum to its maximum value. A look-up table can then be used to colour the AVO, mirroring the variation of the data value assigned to this attribute. The distribution of data along the chosen line or curve is termed a colour map and it can be linear, that is, equal distances along the line correspond to equal increments in data value, or nonlinear. Nonlinear colour maps occur for highlighting tasks, where the aim is to pick out a particular subrange of the data. Linear colour maps occur where the aim is to demonstrate a variable crossing over some significant intermediate value, or to discover the value of a variable at some point(s) on the AVO.

If the task is in some sense to measure data, then complications can arise because, although the colour map may be linear in terms of its construction within the colour model, the same is rarely true of our perceptual response to it. Whilst a model such as HSV allows colours to be described in perceptual terms, we should not make the mistake of assuming it is therefore perceptually uniform. The most striking evidence for this is the colour wheel itself. If the portion corresponding to hue ranging from about 0.16 to 0.5 is mapped linearly to data, narrow bands of yellow and cyan are seen at either end, separated by a much broader band of green (Fig. 4.7). This effect has its roots in the way our cone sensitivities span the wavelengths in the visible spectrum (recall Fig. 4.2). A colour map constructed like this results in good data discrimination at its extremes, but a large number of values in the middle will seem to be equal. The overall effect is thus nonlinear, even though functionally the colour map is linear. This and similar problems could be alleviated by constructing colour maps within a perceptually uniform colour space. These do exist but are rarely found in off-the-shelf visualization tools. Practically, therefore, we have to use models like the ones already described, but with a degree of care. We also have to be aware how anomalous colour vision might affect perception of the chosen colour map. The remainder of this section thus shows some basic colour

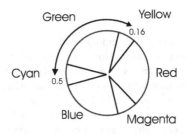

Fig. 4.7. Regions of good hue discrimination (narrow-angle segments) on the colour wheel alternate with portions where many hues appear similar (wide-angle).

mapping strategies, then looks at some perceptual effects and colour vision deficiency.

4.4.1 Nonlinear Colour Mapping

Figure 4.8(a) shows a colour map that varies in hue from green corresponding to the data minimum, through cyan to blue at the data maximum. Although the increments on the data scale are all roughly the same, we see that four segments map to each of green and blue, whilst only two segments map to cyan. The visual effect is shown in Fig. 4.8(b), where it is clear that this colour map will highlight data values around the mean, in the particularly visible colour of cyan. Remaining values, however, will only broadly be distinguished as below (green) and above (blue) this mean. Figure 4.8(c) and (d) demonstrate a similar aim, but now where only values at one end of the data range are of particular interest. This colour map can therefore use a single hue plus a value or saturation variation. Here, the chosen hue is red and saturation varies nonlinearly so as to pick out unusually high values of the variable being studied.

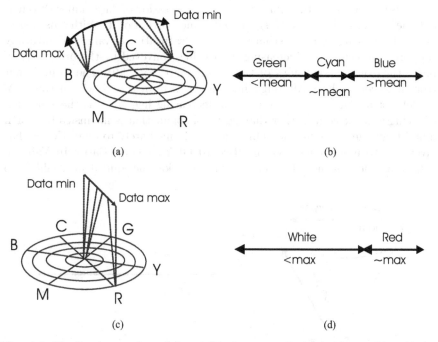

Fig. 4.8. Nonlinear mappings. (a) and (b) show a nonlinear mapping of hues from green to blue that allows values around the mean to be highlighted. (c) and (d) show a nonlinear mapping of one hue from very pale to fully saturated that allows unusually high values to be highlighted.

So where might these types of colour map be used? The first type is used where data points clustered around some special value are of particular interest, and others need to be distinguished but their precise value is not an issue. Visualization of product tolerances falls into this category: those artefacts meeting the acceptance criteria fall into the cyan band and are very obvious; others falling above and below are discounted and their particular value is not important because they will be rejected anyway. What is important, namely the proportion that are above and below the required tolerance, is captured by the colour map because this might give a clue how to alter the production parameters in order to increase usable yield.

The second type of colour map will find extreme values. For instance, particularly high flow rates in a river system might show regions that are prone to scouring of the bed. Giving unremarkable colours (here, white) to all the other, more acceptable, data values concentrates attention on potential problem areas.

4.4.2 'Linear' Colour Mapping

Measurement tasks in visualization differ from the highlighting tasks of the previous section, since the aim is to show a progression of data values throughout the range, rather than to single out some portion of it. With this aim in mind, choosing a colour map that increases in saturation or value will naturally support a perception of increasing data value, conveyed by the progressively purer tints or lighter shades of the colour map (Fig. 4.9). The same is not true, however, of hue. Although hue increases from 0 to 1 within the HSV model just as value and saturation do, increasing hue gives us the sensation of seeing a new colour, rather than seeing a colour that is intrinsically 'worth more' than the previous one. This inability immediately to quantify hue has given rise to mnemonics such as 'Richard Of York Gave Battle In Vain' to help recall the sequence of colours. In visualization the equivalent would be to

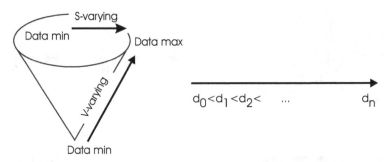

Fig. 4.9. Varying value or saturation will naturally convey a sense of one data value greater than another, though the same is not true for the hues, whose sequence generally has to be learned via a mnemonic such as 'Richard Of York Gave Battle In Vain'.

provide a colour legend (and this is always good practice, no matter what variation is chosen), but the inference of a data value that is mapped to hue will always involve an interpretation step that is largely not needed in saturation- or value-varying schemes. For this reason, even leaving aside the perceptual nonlinearity shown in Fig. 4.7, hue-varying schemes with large numbers of colours should be avoided if the aim is to quantify data, though the many hues will give an overall impression of regions of change if that is all that is required.

Whilst many hues within a single colour map are best avoided, mapping data to smaller hue variations can be quite successful, though only in those regions where our hue discrimination is good (recall Fig. 4.7). If the hues chosen are not particularly suggestive of the variable being displayed then it will still be necessary to learn the sequence, but recalling the order of, say, three hues is much easier than when there are six or seven. As always, a colour legend will support the association until it is memorised sufficiently to make the interpretation step transparent to the visualization user.

A special case of a hue-varying colour map is shown in Fig. 4.10, which demonstrates blending from one hue to another via the line of greys. The middle point, where hue is undefined, is used to signify a cross-over, and increasingly saturated colour demonstrates the 'distance' a value lies from this point. In this example the base hues are red and blue, with a constant green component to take the line through the cube diagonal. It is thus convenient to construct this colour map using RGB parameters (a), rather than HSV as the examples so far have done. As always, though, there is an equivalent description using HSV, but it appears a little more complicated (b) than the single straight-line representation that the RGB model affords.

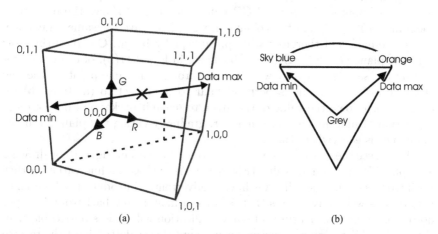

Fig. 4.10. Every colour map will have an equivalent description in terms of RGB and HSV, but may be simpler to construct using one rather than the other set of parameters.

Such a colour map is used to denote values above and below zero or some other, especially significant value. This particular combination of colours is suggestive of a temperature variation below and above ambient, since it is natural to associate blues with cold and reds with hot. Although exactly the same variation could have been achieved with a different hue pair, such as green and magenta, the association with hot and cold would then have required learning, as described earlier. A natural association is thus always worth aiming for, though some variables are more suggestive than others of particular colours.

4.4.3 Perceptual Effects and Colour Vision Deficiency

Our nonlinear hue discrimination mentioned earlier is one consequence of how the cone sensitivities span the visible spectrum. Another is our overall spectral sensitivity, which also has a nonlinear variation with wavelength, the response being greatest in the mid-range and least at the extremes. The effect of this is to make a greenish colour appear brighter to an observer than the equivalent source of red or blue, with blue appearing the least bright.

How bright a colour seems is a subjective quality but we can get a quantitative handle on it by calculating its luminance, Y. For a modern monitor emitting light at the principal wavelengths of its red, green, and blue primaries, the luminance of a particular colour is a weighted sum of its components R, G, and B:

$$Y = 0.2126R + 0.7152G + 0.0722B, \tag{4.1}$$

where we can see from the large 'green' coefficient that this component contributes most to how bright a colour will appear. This equation denotes a sequence of planes within the RGB cube: Fig. 4.11(a) shows the one corresponding to $Y = 0.5$. All the colours on this plane have the same luminance, set at one-half, and therefore will appear equally bright. Compare this now with the plane $(R + G + B)/3 = 0.5$, shown in Fig. 4.11(b), of colours representing the same physical power. It goes through the same point on the line of greys as $Y = 0.5$ but is perpendicular to it. To get to (a) from (b) we have to push down the value of the green to make it darker and decrease the saturation of magenta to make it paler, gradually tilting the plane until the luminance is everywhere the same.

We can see the effect for the colour map put forward in Fig. 4.10 by drawing a graph of Y versus data value (Fig. 4.12). As well as the hue variation that we introduced intentionally, we have inadvertently introduced a luminance variation as well. This means that, against a lighter grey background (upper dotted line) the 'hot' features of our visualization will be less noticeable than the 'cold', whilst against a darker background (lower dotted line) the reverse will be true. Proportionately, the differences diminish against very dark or very light backgrounds, but the effectiveness of a visualization should not on principle depend on such an arbitrary choice. Fortunately for these two hues

the effect is easily corrected by varying the green component a little, and
Fig. 4.13 shows the new and old loci of colours within the RGB cube.

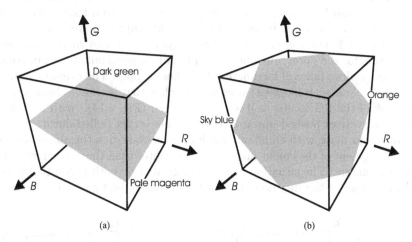

(a)   (b)

Fig. 4.11. In (a) planes of equiluminant colours lie tilted to the line of greys because
the coefficients of the colours' red, green, and blue components are unequal (4.1); in
(b) planes of constant $(R + G + B)/3$, by contrast, lie perpendicular.

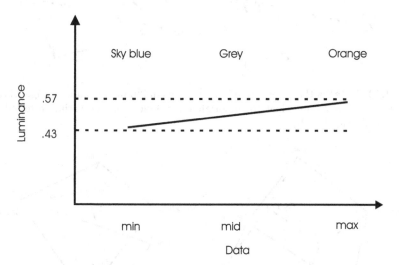

Fig. 4.12. Plot of luminance for a colour map that varies linearly from $(0, 0.5, 1)$
at the minimum data value to $(1, 0.5, 0)$ at the maximum.

Our nonlinear response to wavelength also affects the number of shades and tints that we can distinguish for different hues. For example yellow, being an intrinsically bright hue, makes a much more discriminating value-varying colour map than blue, whilst the converse is true, but to a lesser extent, for a saturation-varying map. It follows that if we attempt to increase the usable range of a single-hue colour map by first varying value and then saturation, the position for the pure, full-value hue will not in general fall at the midpoint, and where it does fall will be different for different hues. The overall dynamic range of a colour map likewise varies with the hue that is chosen. In effect, we can think of the RGB cube as if it were distorted (Fig. 4.14), with its yellow and green vertices pushed upwards and the blue vertex pulled down.

For colour maps with an intentional luminance variation the aim should be for each segment of the colour map to appear lighter than the one before it, by an equal amount. The situation here is complicated by both perceptual issues and the set-up of the monitor's contrast, brightness, and gamma correction.

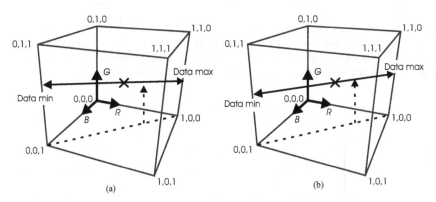

Fig. 4.13. In (a) is the colour map lying on the equiluminant plane of Fig. 4.11(a) that is the nearest equivalent to the original sky blue – orange variation found on the plane of Fig. 4.11(b).

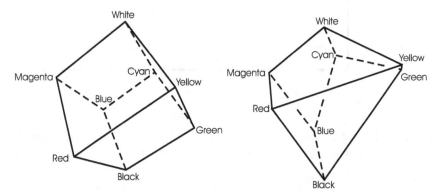

Fig. 4.14. The RGB cube distorted to give an impression of how we see it.

A useful check is always first to display a grey scale to confirm that variation is even across the range: the mid-tones should appear neither too dark nor too light; the scale's black and white endpoints should not 'swallow' a disproportionate range of the data values. Once the grey scale has been checked the colour mapping can proceed to add hue variation. This dependence on the output device underlines a point that is often missed by visualization users, namely that any colour map devised via RGB or HSV is specific to the monitor it was created on. Changing the device will produce a change in appearance even though the map's description has not changed, simply because a colour model makes no reference to the wavelengths of the particular primaries that are used. The potential risk in this can be underestimated – many a visualization presentation has been ruined or had its impact greatly reduced by forgetting to test the colour map that was constructed in the laboratory on the video projector used for the talk.

The device used for the visualization is just one aspect of variation that must be taken into account – another is the user themselves. Adjustment of the colour map will be necessary for users with anomalous colour vision, and for them a completely different strategy might be appropriate. For these users it is important to recall that two of their cone sensitivity curves have reduced (or effectively no) separation (see Sect. 4.2). Precisely that portion of the hue disk between red and green that offers such good discrimination for others will give very little discrimination for the most common colour anomalies. An alternative scheme that involves just one of these hues plus the short-wavelength ('blue') system may have to be substituted. For some types of colour anomaly, reds may already appear dark and therefore a value-varying scheme using low hue angle will be of little value. If only one hue is being used, then effectively its contribution is only to label data, for example, denoting undesirable values in red (Fig. 4.8(d)). In this situation a grey scale could be substituted provided the direction of variation is clear. Even amongst users with normal colour vision it will be necessary to adjust a colour map to help a particular individual understand her data. The strategies presented here should therefore be regarded only as starting points; after all, as Chap. 1 described, the interactive nature of visualization is one aspect that sets it apart from computer graphics, and interaction with colour is simply one facet of this.

Problems

4.1. Describe the process by which we see the yellow colour of a streetlamp. How is it different from seeing the yellow colour of a photograph of a streetlamp displayed on your computer monitor?

4.2. Run the provided software[2] demonstrating the relationship between the RGB and HSV colour models. Rotate the solid, coloured cube so that you are looking down on the white vertex, then turn the solid cube off. You should be looking into the mouth of a six-sided cone; all the points on this cone represent colours whose saturation is one-half. The square-shaped surface represents colours whose value is one-half. Experiment with the saturation and value widgets. Where are the fully saturated colours? Where are the full-value colours?

Use the software to follow the derivation in Sect. 4.3.3 of dark red and pale green. Derive the RGB equivalents of some more complicated colours such as dark yellow and pale magenta.

4.3. Run the provided software demonstrating the use of vector colouring. This is quite a commonly seen technique – the nightly television weather forecast may well use the direction and sizes of its arrows to indicate wind speed and heading, with the colours of the arrows also indicating air temperature. In the example here, two renderings are shown of the same data – the task is to decide whether the flow is predominantly upwards or down. Try adjusting the grey of the background on one of the renderings, making it alternately lighter and darker. What effect do you see and how would you explain it?

4.4. Run the provided software demonstrating the relationship between luminance and RGB value. Locate the colour map shown in Fig. 4.13(a) that runs from sky blue through to orange via equiluminant grey. What is the saturation and value of these endpoint colours? Locate the colour map that runs orthogonal to this one, linking pale-ish magenta with darkish green. Estimate the RGB values of the endpoints of this colour map and put them into (4.1) to confirm that luminance remains constant at one-half.

Construct a colour map linking dark yellow and pale blue that has luminance constant throughout at one-half. This colour map lies on a line halfway between the two already described. Use this colour map in the software supporting Prob. 4.3 in place of the one provided originally and adjust the grey of the background as before. What effect do you see and how would you explain it?

---

[2] The Preface contains details of where to obtain the software that supports the problems.

5

Choosing Techniques

This chapter puts forward a matching method for choosing techniques based on the one hand on a classification of the data and, on the other, taxonomy of currently available techniques.

5.1 Classifying Data

Section 2.2.2 introduced the notion of what is underlying data and mentioned interpolation as a means of filling in the gaps. In this section we re-visit this idea in a little more detail in order to define some necessary terminology for describing data.

5.1.1 Dependent and Independent Variables

Modelling what is underlying data is important because a table of numbers only contains samples of what is being looked at, from which we must reconstruct an object that is representative of the whole. Take, for example, the simple formula

$$y = 2x + 1. \tag{5.1}$$

This is a particular case of $y = ax + b$, where a and b are constants. This line must intercept the y-axis (where $x = 0$) at b and similarly must intercept the x-axis at $x = -b/a$. The gradient, or slope, of any such line is thus always $b \div b/a = a$. Having worked out the particular values of intercept and slope for (5.1) we could therefore draw the corresponding line graph as in Fig. 5.1(a). We could also have arrived at this visualization another way, though, using computed values such as in Table 5.1. Plotting these is, of course, highly indicative of a linear relation and, having taken a few measurements to determine the intercept and slope, we may well propose to interpolate the points (Fig. 5.1(b)) using (5.1).

The difference between these two scenarios is that the first is a mathematical description that is known to be valid for all values of x, whereas the second is a numerical description defined only at discrete points. In scientific visualization the second scenario is the one more commonly found, with data only available at certain points. The reason for this is that computational science usually sets out with a mathematical formulation of a problem but typically the equations are too hard to solve outright over the whole range of the variables. Breaking down into smaller chunks and solving numerically is often the only option, making it necessary to try to work backwards to what the answer would have been had the problem been solvable in the first place. For this example, then, the proposed model of the answer is $y = ax + b$ with $a = 2$ and $b = 1$. Having one model fit the whole range of the variables is rare – it is more usual to need one per chunk – but it will suffice for current purposes.

Table 5.1. Values of y that satisfy (5.1) for various values of x

			$y = 2x + 1$		
x	1	2	3	4	5
y	3	5	7	9	11

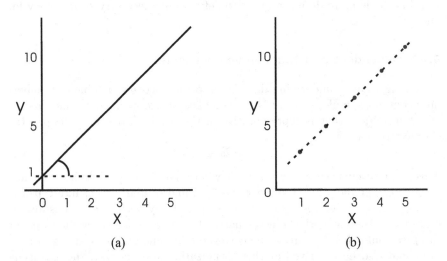

(a)   (b)

Fig. 5.1. In (a), a line drawn with a particular intercept and slope defines a relation between x and y that is valid everywhere. By contrast in (b), plotting individual values from Table 5.1 may be highly suggestive of the same relation, but we will never really know if our guesswork between the points and beyond them is valid.

The first element of terminology to master in computational science (and therefore in scientific visualization) is the concept of dependent and independent variables. Here we have two variables (remember a and b are constants) x and y. Variable x is called the independent variable because it is the one we choose to set the value of (vary independently) before solving for y, written on its own on the left of the 'equals'. Variable y, because its value depends on that chosen for x, is termed the dependent variable. In fact, because this relation is linear we could rearrange the equation and then choose any y in order to solve for x, i.e., $x = (y - b)/a$. Although the numbers in the table would coincide if we happened to choose the same points as before, the variables in this case would switch roles: y would now be the independent variable and x, because its value is calculated from y's, would become the dependent variable. If we were to plot this new function we would switch the axes, too, because conventionally the vertical direction is used for the dependent variable and the horizontal for the independent. Switching axes like this could well generate confusion though, because the one usually called y would be labelled x, and vice versa.

This discussion shows up two drawbacks in this way of writing mathematical relationships: firstly, (5.1) is immediately suggestive of a line graph, indeed, the name sometimes given to this technique is an 'x-y' plot. Secondly, the idea of plotting a relation between x and y is so bound up with the line graph it leads to assumptions, which as we have seen might not be valid, about which variable is dependent and which independent.

What is needed is an AVO-independent notation that also makes clear which is the dependent and which the independent variable. Rewriting (5.1) as

$$f(x) = 2x + 1 \qquad\qquad (5.2)$$

solves both these problems. $f(x)$, meaning "function of x", unambiguously distinguishes this quantity as the dependent variable, whilst the x within the brackets shows that this variable, wherever it occurs in the formula, can never be anything other than the independent one. The same understanding would hold even if we were to rearrange to give $x = (f(x) - 1)/2$, $1 = f(x) - 2x$, or any other version we could think of.

Thinking about data in the abstract like this, without preconceptions as to how we will display it, can also be beneficial when it comes to choosing techniques. For instance, having broken the inherent association of the dependent variable with the y-axis of a line graph we might now think of mapping this data instead to the loudness or pitch of a sound generated as we move a probe back and forth along a line denoting the independent variable. We will also find an abstract approach is of value when considering higher-dimensional data, and when reducing data dimensions by taking slices or sections. Further details will be given in Sect. 5.1.3.

By extending the notation of (5.2) a little we can also distinguish whether we are dealing with a mathematical model that is valid over the whole range of the independent variables or a numerical one valid only at discrete points. Generally $f(x)$ is taken to mean the former and f_x the latter. Thus, from Table 5.1 we would deduce $f_1 = 3$, $f_2 = 5$ and so on.

So much for the concept of independent and dependent variables when the model is a mathematical one. This situation obviously covers simulation data, but Sect. 3.1 talked of other types of data too, such as scanner output and experimental results. Does the idea extend naturally to these other types? Fortunately the answer is 'yes', provided we hold onto the principle of choosing one value (the independent variable) in order to find the other (the dependent variable). Thus, in the case of the scanner output of Sect. 3.1 we can think of choosing a particular coordinate in the person's head in order to measure the tissue density there. Needless to say, a CT scanner doesn't quite work like this, but the metaphor is useful here. The independent variable is the place we choose to make the measurement and the dependent variable is the value we find there. For the combustion chamber of Fig. 2.20 the independent variable is time, because we choose the times at which to monitor the chamber and the equipment reading tells us the ozone concentration. The ozone concentration value thus goes up or down depending on when we read it. To emphasise the dependence on time we could model this system as "$f(t)$" rather than "$f(x)$". Here we see another advantage of thinking about data in the abstract: even though the experiment never existed as a mathematical formulation originally, referring to "$f(t)$" is still a convenient way of capturing what we are trying to reconstruct. What follows will thus refer to any data using the "function of" notation, whether or not it is the result of a simulation, measurement or experiment.

5.1.2 Data Domain

Having arrived at the idea of a model, $f(x)$, of what is underlying data, we need now to generalise. Our first observation relates to the independent variable x, which we can see from Table 5.1 is not just a set of numbers but a *sequence* of numbers. In fact, x is more properly described as a vector quantity, that is, it consists of both a magnitude and a direction defined according to some coordinate system. We could be forgiven for not recognising it as such in this case, because the coordinate system is just a single straight line with the various data points marked off along it. Since the line is one-dimensional we can refer to this data as having a 1D domain or, even more succinctly, as "1D data".

Vectors are usually depicted in bold upright face to distinguish them from ordinary quantities, therefore our model is not just $f(x)$ but strictly $f(\mathbf{x})$. Given an appropriate coordinate system it could therefore also describe 2D, 3D or even nD data. If the data is time-varying as well, this dimension is not usually folded in with $\mathbf{x}$ but written as $f(\mathbf{x}; t)$. The fact that we are not restricted to three dimensions (plus time, if present) when talking about the data domain represents another generalisation. Whilst it is true we can only readily conceive of *visualizations* occupying three-dimensional space, the same is not true of *data*. However, if we do ever meet data of higher dimension than three, we have to think in terms of projections or slices in order to overcome the natural limitations of our perceptual abilities.

As data grows in the number of its dimensions, so too does the available choice of coordinate system. Most readers will be familiar with Cartesian co-ordinates defined on two or three mutually perpendicular axes. These axial systems are very useful for describing problems over a rectangular domain but they are by no means the only ones available and others can be more conve-nient if they match the geometry of the problem better. Polar coordinates are commonly encountered: Fig. 5.2 shows cylindrical and spherical polar coordi-nate systems, which might respectively be used for describing flow in a pipe and convection physics within the Sun. Both these problems would be much harder to define and solve in rectangular coordinates. When visualizing the results, however, it may well be necessary to transform to a Cartesian system because this is what most off-the-shelf software employs.

After the separation of the independent from the dependent variables, the identification of the data domain as 1D, 2D, and so on is the next most important step in choosing an appropriate visualization technique. The par-ticular coordinate system used is not usually a complicating factor in this, since transformation between coordinate systems of equivalent dimension is always possible. Data that is 3D, for example, in one coordinate system will remain 3D in any it is re-described for. These cases are therefore straightfor-

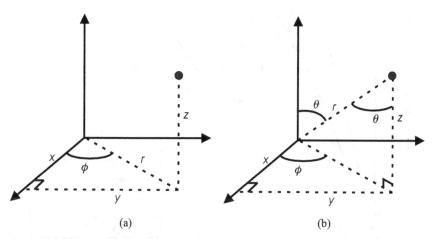

(a)   (b)

Fig. 5.2. In (a), a point whose cylindrical polar coordinates are (r, ϕ, z) has an equivalent description in Cartesian coordinates $(x, y, z) = (r \cos \phi, r \sin \phi, z)$. In (b) the same point described in spherical polar coordinates as (r, θ, ϕ) corresponds to $(x, y, z) = (r \sin \theta \cos \phi, r \sin \theta \sin \phi, r \cos \theta)$. It is easy to see that setting $z = 0$ in (a) or $\theta = \pi/2$ in (b) yields a single 2D polar system (r, ϕ) where $(x, y) = (r \cos \phi, r \sin \phi)$.

ward to classify. Care is needed, however, when we encounter a data domain embedded within a space of higher dimension, since it is the dimension of the domain itself that determines the techniques we will use, not the dimension of the enclosing space. Such data is said to be defined on a manifold, that is, a structure that locally appears to be of lower dimension than it does globally. Our very own Earth is perhaps one of the best illustrations of the concept of a manifold – from space it appears three-dimensional but on its surface we navigate in terms of two variables, latitude and longitude. When we visualize the height of the land or rainfall across the region we therefore choose from the techniques available for 2D data, not those for 3D, because the domain is inherently two-dimensional. Section 5.1.3 illustrates these principles further.

5.1.3 Scalar and Vector Types

The discussion of Sect. 5.1.2 deals with the independent variable; our next generalisation concerns the dependent variable and its qualities. The $f(\mathbf{x})$ we have met thus far is a single-valued quantity, or scalar function, but there could be several relations like this involving $\mathbf{x}$ that are true simultaneously. We can thus imagine two scalar dependent variables $f(\mathbf{x})$ and $g(\mathbf{x})$ defined across the domain which might be plotted as multiple line graphs (Fig. 5.3).

Multiple scalar dependent variables are perfectly common but let us now suppose that the independent variable of Fig. 5.3 is time and f and g are

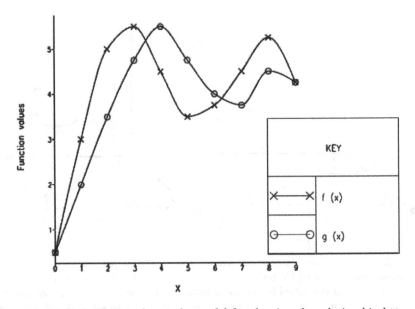

Fig. 5.3. Multiple line graphs can be useful for showing the relationship between several scalar values across the same data domain. Image credit: IRIS Explorer, synthetic data.

the Cartesian coordinates of an insect as it scurries around the floor. Plotting its path (Fig. 5.4) gives us a quite different visualization to the multiple line graphs but one which is much more illuminating, since now it is obvious the ant spends much of its time in the top right corner of the space. Rather than having dependent variables that are two separate scalars, this data is really a single dependent variable that is a two-dimensional vector. Mostly we think of vectors when the problem is one of fluid flow, such as in weather forecasting or when charting ocean currents. Talking of positions as vectors might thus be an unfamiliar concept but we can see they are so when we look at the essential rôle of the coordinate system in making sense of the f and g: had these been equivalent to the r and ϕ of a polar coordinate system (see Fig. 5.2), then the ant's path would have been very different.

In fact, we can tie up this example with the concept of manifolds introduced earlier. Looking at the path in Fig. 5.4 from the ant's point of view, it is one-dimensional because locally there is just where he is headed and where he's been. From our elevated position, however, we see the global picture of his route embedded in two-dimensional space. If the ant is being monitored at time intervals Δt, we see that the independent variable, time, is spread out along the insect's path. This is entirely consistent because time is one-dimensional, just as the path is when it is viewed locally. Widely separated points occur in high-speed regions, where the magnitude of the ant's velocity is greatest. We could therefore have converted this data to a set of velocity

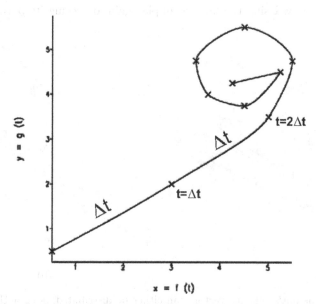

Fig. 5.4. The same data as in Fig. 5.3 looks rather different when it is interpreted as position vectors observed at time intervals Δt. Image credit: IRIS Explorer, synthetic data.

vectors and viewed them either along a 1D time axis as in Fig. 5.5(a) or distributed according to the ant's current position as in Fig. 5.5(b).

Whether we talk of position vectors or velocity vectors, this problem's dependent variable is described in terms of a set of two-dimensional axes for the vectors attached at every point on the 1D axis of the time-line comprising the independent variable (Fig. 5.6). This figure underlines an important point about dependent and independent variables, namely that the coordinate system that defines the one need not be the same as that for the other. Scalar data across a 2D domain, for instance, comprises a one-dimensional dependent variable axis (the real number line) attached at every point of the (higher-dimensioned) 2D data domain. In vector problems the reverse is often seen, with a dependent variable space of higher dimension than the data domain. This is a feature not only of trajectories but also occurs in 3D fluid flow problems when the domain is sliced to reduce the amount of data being handled. The slicing operation reduces the dimension of the independent variable to 2D but the dependent variable is unaffected – each 2D slice still contains three-dimensional vectors. Stacking the slices back up again in order restores the volume to its original form.

Distinguishing whether a dependent variable should be treated as multiple scalars or an n-dimensional vector is occasionally a matter of interpretation but what should never be in doubt is the separation of the independent from the dependent variables. The concept of which to choose and which to determine holds fast whatever complications are brought on by the spaces the variables occupy. Using the 'ant' example again, on seeing its path we could

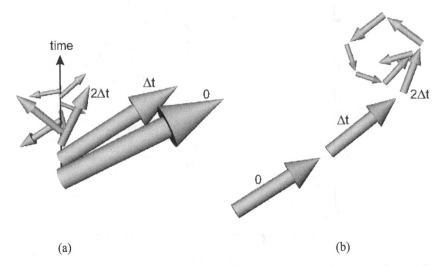

(a)   (b)

Fig. 5.5. The ant's velocity vectors can either be distributed along a 1D time-line pointing into the page (a) or within a plane according to the ant's current position (b). Note how the longer vectors in (b) correspond with more widely separated points in Fig. 5.4.

quite easily have mistaken the two-dimensional space of its position vectors (Fig. 5.4) for the data domain and referred to f and g as the independent variables. After all, in the case of the line graph one of the axes of the visualization object depicted the independent variable, so why should the same not be true of the x- and y-axes of Fig. 5.4? For the ant this cannot be right though: we cannot go to just any place we choose and measure when the ant arrives, because it might never visit that spot. What we can do, however, is choose a time and measure where the ant is. Once again, thinking about data in the abstract, without reference to its visualization, is the key to correct classification.

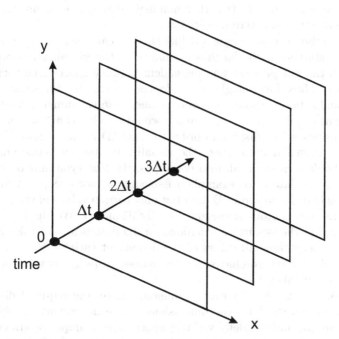

Fig. 5.6. Viewed in the abstract, the 1D time domain of Fig. 5.5(a) has attached to it a sequence of two-dimensional spaces needed to describe the ant's velocities.

5.2 Taxonomy of Visualization Techniques

Having determined the independent and dependent variables of the problem, the dimension of the data domain spanned by the independent variables, and the scalar or vector nature of the dependent variable(s), we are nearly ready to categorise the various techniques we will meet. One final refinement in the description of the independent variable is needed, which is to incorporate the ideas of Sect. 2.2 that distinguished data as nominal, aggregated or ordinal. Recall that nominal (or named) data has no inherent order, though we may choose to display items in a particular sequence to make some special point. Aggregated data occurs where a range of values in the data domain contribute to a single value for the dependent variable that is applicable across the whole of that range. An example would be to visualize the age distribution of the population by counting individuals whose ages fall into a number of 5-year ranges. This type of data must be plotted with the data bins in order, whilst the dependent variable value per bin applies to the whole of that bin. Ordinal data does have an order but may be discontinuous (not join on) from one value to the next. If ordinal data is continuous, it will join on from one value to the next but now we must exercise care when visualizing in how we interpolate, or fill in, between the data points.

Putting all these ideas together yields Table 5.2. Here, the dependent variables and their type(s) determine which column a technique occupies, whilst the dimension and nature (whether nominal, aggregated, or ordinal) of the independent variable determines its row.

When techniques are organised like this we can make some general observations, starting with the dimensionality of the visualization objects in relation to the independent and dependent variable spaces (see Sect. 5.1.3) of the data. Thus, for a single scalar dependent variable the dimensionality of the visualization is usually greater, by one, than the dimensionality of the independent variable space – an example would be a bar chart, which occupies two dimensions of the display in order to show 1D nominal data. Those few techniques for scalar data where the visualization has the same dimensionality as the data domain fall into two types: the first type may only show a selection of the data – for example a flat contour plot occupies two display dimensions in order to show 2D data but only certain values of the dependent variable, i.e. the contour lines, are actually displayed. We shall soon see in Sect. 6.3.2 that the isosurface technique for 3D data is also of this type. The second type may show all values of the dependent variable by using colour; the image display and volume render techniques, respectively used for 2D and 3D data, are of this type.

For vector data the situation is different. Here, the required display dimensions are governed by the dimensions of the dependent variable space rather than the independent variable space. For example, a trajectory of three-dimensional position vectors will yield a line in three dimensions, even though the independent variable, time, is 1D; three-dimensional arrows will

Table 5.2. The visualization techniques that will be described in this book, organised according to the dimension of the data domain and its nature (whether nominal, aggregated, or ordinal), and the number and type(s) of the dependent variable(s)

Independent Variable(s)	Dependent Variable(s)			
	Single Scalar	Multiple Scalars	Vector	Scalar(s) & Vector
1D Nominal	Bar chart	Clustered bar chart Stacked bar chart	Scatterplot	
	Pie chart			
1D Aggregated	Histogram	Superimposed histograms Stacked histograms		
1D Ordinal	Line graph	Superimposed line graphs Stacked line graphs	Trajectory	Coloured trajectory Swept polygon
2D Nominal	2D bar chart			
2D Aggregated	2D histogram Bounded region plot			
2D Ordinal	Image display Contour plot Surface view	Height-field plot	Solid arrows on plane Line arrows Streamline Timeline Flow texture	Coloured arrows Coloured line
3D Ordinal	Isosurface Volume render	Coloured isosurface	Arrows in volume Streamribbon/ surface/tube Time surface	Coloured arrows Swept polygon

require three display dimensions whether they are attached to a plane or sitting within a volume. Colour, if it is used at all with vector techniques, is confined to adding scalar information. We can thus see a pattern developing: data needs a certain number of degrees of freedom to visualize it, which techniques provide by means of their AVOs' spatial and colour attributes. If this book were to deal with perceptualisation the attributes could also include sound (auditory displays), or touch and force-feedback (haptic displays).

Another observation we can make is that not all these attributes are equally in demand when mapping data to features of the AVO: a glance across Table 5.2 shows that spatial features dominate over colour, which tends to be used to add information to an existing visualization object. For example, we would never show 1D ordinal data as a straight but coloured line if we had the option to draw a line graph, but if the line represents an insect's trajectory we may well colour it if we also want to show its speed (a scalar) along the path.

As well as adding desirable information, colour may become an essential device if all the display's available spatial dimensions already hold some special significance. For example, a surface view (recall Fig. 2.10) would be fine for showing, say, temperature across a flat data domain. However if the domain is the curved wing of an aircraft it would be confusing to show the dependent variable as a perpendicular displacement of that curvature, even though this is the exact counterpart of height in a surface view. We would not know, from looking at the visualization object, whether the form of the surface derived from the shape of the wing, the temperature distribution across it, or a combination of both. In this case we would use the spatial degrees of freedom solely to describe the wing shape – a 2D domain embedded in three-dimensional space – and then construct an overlay of colours or greyscale (an image display) on this manifold. Draping an initially flat contour plot over the wing shape would achieve much the same purpose.

The essence of the difficulty just described is how to maintain uniqueness of data-to-attribute mapping. A similar problem arises if the domain is sliced to reduce its dimensions. Recall from Sect. 5.1.3 that the slicing operation reduces the dimension of the independent variable but leaves the dependent variable space unchanged. We could therefore imagine augmenting the techniques shown in Table. 5.2 for 3D scalar data by taking slices of the volume and applying techniques for 2D data to them. Image displays (recall Fig. 2.14) and contour plots would be good candidates because they can show 2D data within two display dimensions. However, surface views would have restricted utility in this situation since they need a third display dimension, potentially becoming confused with the third domain dimension that is orthogonal to the slice.

Slicing the domain progressively reduces the dimension of the independent variable, moving up the rows of the table. The opposite operation, stacking, takes us down the rows, and usually warrants consideration when data sets are time-varying. Whilst the obvious suggestion for showing time-varying data is to animate the equivalent static visualization, whether to map time to animation or space can in fact depend on the intended medium and whether the display's spatial degrees of freedom are already used up. Thus, Fig. 2.13 showed the individual frames from a visualization designed to show 2D time-varying data as an animated surface view. Since one surface view already occupies three dimensions of the display there are only two options: either tile the multiple surface views or animate them. The same would not be true of 1D time-varying data, though. Whilst it would be possible to animate a line graph, or tile a set of line graphs, we could also consider stacking up the frames to make a static 2D domain and applying a surface view. In this way the complete variation is captured in one, stationary display. Mapping to space like this, rather than animation, is also the preferred option when time is the only independent variable: a line graph whose x-axis denotes time is much more useful than animating a single point back and forth along a line denoting the numerical range of the dependent variable.

As well as denoting time, animation can also be used for static data if the visualization technique can only cover part of the domain at any one moment. Slicing a volume and applying techniques for 2D data as was just described has a drawback: more slices cover the volume better but make it more difficult to see between them. Another solution, described in Sect. 2.1.3, was to animate a single slice back and forth. In terms of Table 5.2, animation can therefore fulfill a dual rôle: it can be mapped by the independent variable 'time' or provide another degree of freedom to help visualize a static data set. Needless to say it should not be asked to do both simultaneously, for that would violate the uniqueness principle!

The remainder of this book now goes into more detail on the construction and usage of each visualization. Chapter 6 deals with purely scalar data and the techniques in the first two columns of Table 5.2. Chapter 7 completes the table by covering vector data and, where applicable, the addition of scalar information.

Problems

5.1. Go back through all the figures so far in this book that show a visualization and see if you can classify the data for each one in terms of its independent and dependent variable(s), and whether they are scalar or vector type.

5.2. Early map-makers used to draw terrain in pseudo-perspective in order to convey the idea of rising and falling ground. As a technique it had some advantages in that hills were immediately distinguishable from valleys, but disadvantages in the degree of accuracy with which the different heights and their horizontal location could be conveyed. This pictorial approach has almost universally fallen into disuse, except for some city tourist maps that sometimes depict landmarks in this way.

Given a table of values representing a terrain as heights above sea level, what are the dependent and independent variables of this problem? What is the usual representation of such data in

1. a rambler's map of the countryside
2. a page in an atlas?

5.3. A common technique for showing pressure on a weather map is to use isobars. Classify this data in terms of its independent and dependent variables. What is the generic name of the technique being used?

5.4. Arrows are frequently used to show wind speed and direction on a weather map. Does adding colour to the arrows to signify how warm or cold the air is affect the classification of the independent or the dependent variables?

6

Visualizing Scalars

The previous chapter introduces the notion of the different degrees of freedom provided by the attributes of abstract visualization objects, together with some rules of thumb that help distribute features in data onto these attributes. This chapter now looks at the use of each technique for scalar data in turn, gradually working down the rows of Table 5.2. The large-scale organisation of the chapter thus reflects the dimension of the data domain, i.e., the independent variable. Within this overall approach, techniques for nominal and aggregated data are described first, followed by those for ordinal data. Since ordinal data may be continuous across the domain it requires a framework over which we can interpolate, so triangulation of 2D and 3D data is described at the appropriate point in each section.

6.1 1D Data

A number of techniques for 1D data with a single scalar variable have already been encountered in previous chapters and the principles described there need not be revisited. Looking at Table 5.2, however, it is noticeable that 1D data differs from 2D and 3D in the possibilities available to display several scalars simultaneously. In this section we therefore concentrate on some strategies for displaying multiple scalar values defined over a 1D domain.

6.1.1 Bar Chart, Pie Chart, and Scatterplot

Two common strategies for handling multiple scalars within a bar chart are first to cluster and second to stack the bars, as shown in Figs. 6.1 and 6.2. Clustering (also called grouping) emphasises variation between dependent variables whereas stacking emphasises variation within each one. A problem with stacking the bars is that each scalar is added to the one before it so the success of this type of display is very much dependent on the degree of variation to be shown and on the order of placing the components. In Fig. 6.2(a) the variable placed first increases a little and then falls back to slightly less than the leftmost value. The next variable, forming the middle of the stacks, exhibits similar properties which further magnifies the rise in the baseline on which the third set is placed. This set is different to the first two, exhibiting a fall first and then a rise, a variation that is quite difficult to spot when the eye is more naturally drawn to the endpoints of the bars. Figure 6.2(b) reverses the order of placement of the components. The distinctive variation of the third set of scalars is now easy to see but possibly at the expense of understanding the others as well as we did with (a).

For all its faults, bar stacking is very useful for showing the variation of summed scalars, something that a clustered chart does not easily convey. If the requirement, however, is to show values as a proportion of the total then in limited circumstances a pie chart may be more effective. Figure 6.3 compares a bar chart with a pie chart of the same set of data and the latter does give a sense of each value contributing proportionately to the whole. The effectiveness of pie charts in scaling up to multiple dependent variables is debatable, though – tiling the different charts is an obvious choice but their effective comparison introduces the conflicting requirement for proximity on the display.

If a dataset is large and has multiple scalar dependent variables, then a scatterplot is worth considering. Figure 6.4 shows a three-dimensional scatterplot, where the coordinates of each of the n points are obtained from the corresponding dependent variables, i.e., $(x, y, z)_n = (var1, var2, var3)_n$. Clustering of points into a group, or onto a line or plane in the space, shows a relationship between the dependent variables that might not be seen with a stacked or clustered bar chart.

A potential confusion that is worth mentioning here arises in respect of the axis labels of Fig. 6.4, all of which reflect the names of the dependent variables. The names comprising the individual independent variable values, which in a bar chart would appear below the bars, now apply to the individual points in the scatterplot. These might be drawn by means of text labels that float alongside in the three-dimensional space, though cluttering of the display can be a problem. A scatterplot can thus show a correlation between multiple

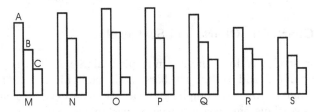

Fig. 6.1. A clustered bar chart emphasises the variation between the dependent variables.

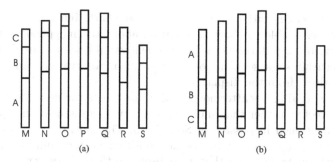

Fig. 6.2. Compared with Fig. 6.1, stacking bars emphasises variation within each variable, though the insight gained is dependent on the data and the order of stacking.

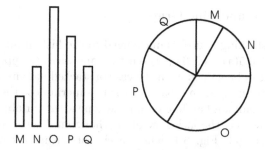

Fig. 6.3. The same data can be displayed using a bar chart and a pie chart. In a bar chart the relative sizes of the values are easily judged, but in a pie chart their contribution as a proportion of the whole is emphasised.

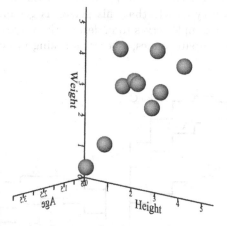

Fig. 6.4. A three-dimensional scatterplot showing the relationship between dependent variable values of height, weight, and age observed for 10 different individuals. Image credit: IRIS Explorer, synthetic data.

dependent variables rather better than a bar chart, but somewhat at the expense of being able to show information about the independent variable. Fortunately, for large datasets the independent variable values are often simply identifiers within some sequence of experiments or observations, and might be omitted entirely from the display.

Strictly speaking a scatterplot visualization treats the dependent variable as a single vector, rather than multiple scalar type, an issue of interpretation that was mentioned in passing in Sect. 5.1.3. The individual values become the different components of the points' position vectors and we can see a parallel with the trajectories that were discussed there. However, because the independent variable is nominal there are no connections between the points because the data has no inherent order.

6.1.2 Histogram and Line Graph

The concept of stacking transfers unchanged to the histogram and line graph techniques (Figs. 6.5(a) and 6.6(a)) but the same caveats apply in respect of the insight that can be gained as in the case of stacked bar charts. The closest analogue of clustering bars in a bar chart is to superimpose the different lines since this uses a common baseline for all the dependent variables (Figs. 6.5(b) and 6.6(b)). However, the lack now of any horizontal separation to the different components (cf. Fig. 6.1, where each bar within a cluster remained distinct) may make the variation between several dependent variables harder to understand, especially if the lines criss-cross one another. An important counterexample occurs when the difference between just two variables is what is important – in Fig. 6.7 the increasing distance with time between the two plotted lines shows very clearly that this person is getting further and further into debt. This example serves to underline the value of superimposition (and clustering) to compare values, whereas stacking principally shows their summation.

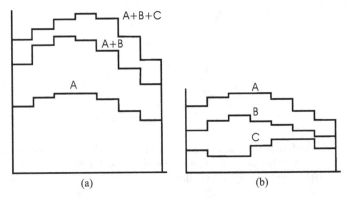

Fig. 6.5. A stacked (a) compared with a superimposed (b) set of histograms.

6.2 2D Data

All of the visualizations in Sect. 6.1 occupied two display dimensions. For 2D scalar data we need three degrees of freedom so we can either use three display dimensions or two display dimensions augmented by colour. Alternatively we might use two display dimensions but show the data selectively. Increasing the dimensionality of the data domain also introduces the possibility of slicing it and applying techniques from Sect. 6.1. Similarly we shall see under what conditions it may be feasible to stack several 1D data domains in order to apply the techniques in this section.

6.2.1 2D Bar Chart

For 2D data the bar chart technique extends quite naturally, with three-dimensional bars set perpendicular to the base plane of the visualization. If there are several scalars, then stacking and clustering can theoretically be used as for 1D data, but in practice the problems of occlusion and clutter make interpretation very difficult. Even with just one scalar the price paid for being

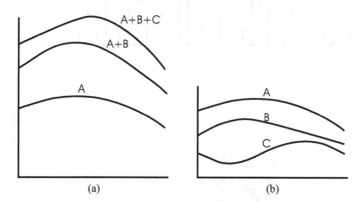

Fig. 6.6. A stacked (a) compared with a superimposed (b) set of line graphs.

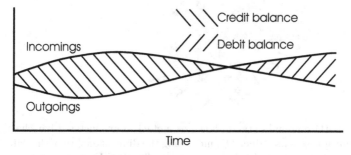

Fig. 6.7. Two superimposed line graphs show very naturally the difference between variables and the variation of this difference across the data domain.

able to see variations according to two independent variables is occlusion. The ability to rotate the visualization interactively is important here, as is the option to turn off perspective projection when trying to make quantitative judgments. Slicing the domain and using the equivalent technique for 1D data (recall Figs. 2.6 and 2.7) will also aid accurate comparison if needed.

A 2D bar chart can also present a means to display 1D nominal data with multiple scalar variables but without having to stack or cluster the bars as was described in Sect. 6.1. Figure 6.8 shows the same data as Figs. 6.1 and 6.2, with the three dependent variables called A, B, and C now having assumed the role of one, new, nominal independent variable with values A, B, and C. In effect, the multiplicity of scalars has been reduced by increasing the dimensionality of the data, a manipulation that is feasible because the domain is nominal. With this three-dimensional representation, variation between the (formerly three dependent) variables is now obtained with one view, whilst variation within them is seen by rotating to look from the orthogonal direction.

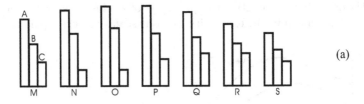

(a)

(b)

Fig. 6.8. A 1D nominal dataset shown as a stacked or clustered bar chart (a) can have its multiple scalars reduced by increasing the dimensionality of the data domain and using a 2D bar chart (b). Lower image credit: IRIS Explorer, synthetic data.

6.2.2 2D Histogram

Transformations of the dependent into independent variables should be undertaken with some care when the data is aggregated. An example can be seen in the visualizations of student marks in Fig. 6.9, where the 'Maths' and 'Physics' dependent variables, whose histograms are superimposed in (a), have been separated and recombined to form a 2D data object. This does not produce a 2D aggregated data domain but rather it results in a hybrid where one independent variable is aggregated and the second is nominal (c). Only (b) in Fig. 6.9 is genuinely a 2D histogram, showing the frequency of marks for Maths *and* Physics simultaneously.

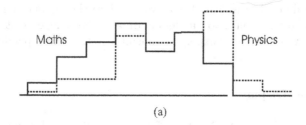

(a)

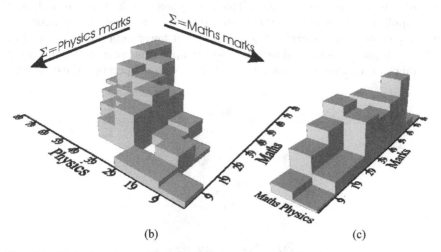

(b)   (c)

Fig. 6.9. Reducing the multiplicity of dependent variables in a superimposed histogram of 1D data (a) results in a hybrid visualization (c). In order to see the variation of the Maths and Physics marks simultaneously (b) we need to reconstruct the data values that were originally summed to produce (a) and (c). Lower images credit: IRIS Explorer, synthetic data.

6.2.3 Bounded Region Plot

A different example of 2D aggregated data occurs where the spatial arrangement of the data domain itself holds some special significance. Now each
dependent variable applies to the whole of a bounded region of the independent variables, which might for example be the collection wards of a census or
the countries in a dominion. Figure 6.10 shows a fictitious dataset where the
number of red cars and the total number of cars have been counted for the
various counties in England, Scotland, and Wales. The data has then been aggregated into a single percentage value for each country and mapped to three
different greyscale values. One problem with this type of plot is that the importance ascribed each region is in proportion to its area and not necessarily
the magnitude of its associated data value. Here then is another example of
a visualization trade-off: good understanding of the independent variable domain possibly comes at the expense of misinterpreting the dependent variable.

6.2.4 Image Display

The last 2D technique we shall meet that does not require interpolation is
an image display, used for large amounts of observational data such as that
recorded by satellites or scanners. This is mapped to colour or greyscale and
then applied pixel-by-pixel to the display. If the data is dense, the visualization
will appear to vary smoothly (Fig. 6.11(a)), but fewer data points mapped to
a larger display area (b) will reveal a 'blocky' appearance caused by allocating
several pixels to the same data value. For this zooming operation the data have

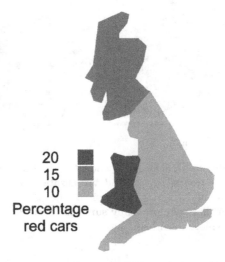

Fig. 6.10. Map of Great Britain shaded to illustrate the individual countries' pref-
erences for red cars. Image credit: IRIS Explorer, synthetic data.

thus been interpreted as discontinuous at each pixel block edge (Fig. 6.12), rather than blending smoothly from one to the next. Had we taken a slice along a row j or column i of pixels and plotted the f_{xj} or f_{iy} as a line graph, it would look like the average monthly share price data of Fig. 2.17.

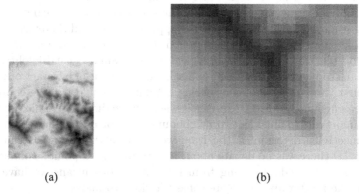

(a)   (b)

Fig. 6.11. Image display showing data mapped to greyscale and plotted (a) with a one-to-one data point to pixel correspondence. In a 'zoom' operation (b), a small portion from the bottom left of (a) is shown with a one-to-many correspondence that leads to a blocky appearance in the visualization. Image credit: IRIS Explorer, test data suite.

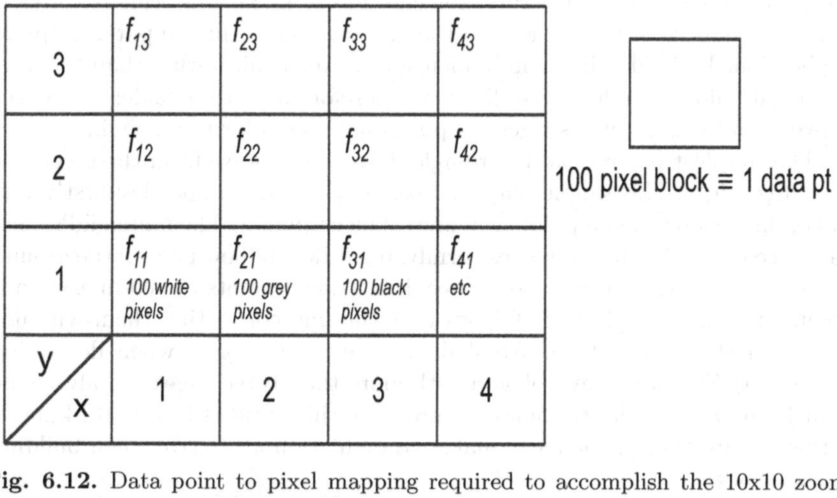

3	f_{13}	f_{23}	f_{33}	f_{43}
2	f_{12}	f_{22}	f_{32}	f_{42}
1	f_{11} 100 white pixels	f_{21} 100 grey pixels	f_{31} 100 black pixels	f_{41} etc
y／x	1	2	3	4

100 pixel block ≡ 1 data pt

Fig. 6.12. Data point to pixel mapping required to accomplish the 10x10 zoom in Fig. 6.11(b). We can think of the data as constant within each pixel block and discontinuous at block edges.

6.2.5 Making a Framework

The remainder of the 2D techniques to be described will involve some form of blending from one data point to another. Building a framework is our next consideration; it will not only support the interpolation necessary for finding data values in between those that are given but may also be called upon to provide a means of generating the geometry that is output from the mapping stage. As we shall soon see, the appearance of (and therefore possibly the insight conveyed by) the visualization depends on this framework, so its proper construction is yet another aspect of maintaining visual fidelity.

We can stop here for a moment and ask why the issue of a framework arises for the first time only when considering 2D data – should not the equivalent have been encountered in 1D? In fact it was, but we didn't recognise it: inside a 1D domain each point has two neighbours (one for a boundary point) and this connectivity determined the framework for interpolation. Because the data was 1D there was no debate about how to identify a point's connectivity but the greater freedom arising from two dimensions means we have some choice in the matter and therefore some decisions to make.

For gridded data we can take our cue from the 1D case and propose a framework that uses a point's neighbours (Fig. 6.13(a)) to generate a wire-frame. We could even imagine using this framework directly to produce a rudimentary surface, by slicing the domain repeatedly in both the x- and y-directions. Applying a line graph to each subset of the data then gives Fig. 6.13(b) but the value of this plot is rather limited by its see-through nature. Our visual system allows us to perceive depth via a number of mechanisms, one of which is the interposition cue. The brain assigns occluded objects to greater depths in the scene, and the cue is provided in computer graphics applications by hidden line and hidden surface removal. Rather than thinking of the data along a collection of lines, we therefore have to consider the spaces between and this in turn suggests a polygonal model for the domain.

The simplest polygon is the triangle, formed of course from three vertices and three edges. This simple shape has some interesting properties: firstly, any three, three-dimensional points will always be co-planar. The milkmaid's stool has three legs so it will always rest firmly, regardless of how uneven the ground might be. Furthermore any two, three-dimensional points are co-linear[1] so if points are within a plane, it follows that the line connecting them will also lie within this same plane. We shall use this fact shortly when describing contouring. Secondly, any polygon with more than three edges can always be built from two or more triangles. A 'proof' of this appears in Fig. 6.14 and it is this feature that particularly makes triangulation attractive when building a framework.

Figure 6.15 shows some special triangulations that arise for gridded data, which will be used later. In the case of two triangles per grid cell, choosing

---

[1] A two-legged stool would also rest firmly but regrettably comes up short in the stability department.

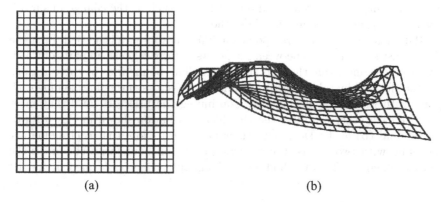

(a)   (b)

Fig. 6.13. Using a point's neighbours will generate a line-based framework (a) but without the means to support hidden line removal (b). Image credit: IRIS Explorer, synthetic data.

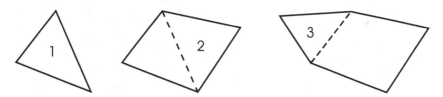

Fig. 6.14. Adding successive triangles increases the number of polygon edges by 2 but at the expense of making an existing edge internal. The overall increase in edges per triangle added is therefore 1, so it follows that triangles can be used to build a polygon with any number of edges ≥ 3.

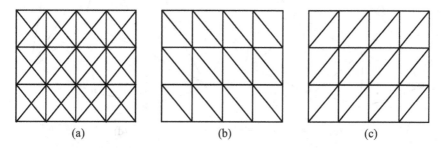

(a)   (b)   (c)

Fig. 6.15. Triangulations of gridded data can consist of 4 (a) or 2 (b, c) triangles per cell. Other combinations of diagonals mixing styles (b) and (c) can also be considered depending how the data varies across the domain.

consistent diagonals leads to (b) or (c) or, if the data is known in advance, a mixture may be selected based on a criterion such as the change in surface normal on going from one triangle to the next.

If data is given at scattered points, a different approach is needed. First the space must be divided up between the points to form regions, all parts of which are closer to one point than all the others. The boundaries of these regions are thus formed by taking the perpendicular bisectors of the lines joining each point with its nearest neighbours. Continuing the bisectors until they meet up with each other produces the Dirichlet tessellation shown in Fig. 6.16(a), whose dual (b) is the Delaunay triangulation (c). Note that each boundary meets up with two others; the collection of region boundaries comprises the Voronoi diagram. This method avoids long, thin triangles formed by having

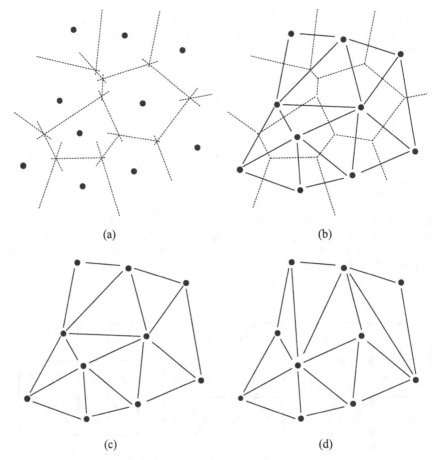

(a)   (b)

(c)   (d)

Fig. 6.16. The Dirichlet tessellation (a) is dual (b) with the Delaunay triangulation (c), which provides vertex connectivity avoiding long, thin triangles (d).

one angle very different to the other two; one example for this set of data points appears in (d).

6.2.6 Contour Plot

Drawing a contour depends on finding the set of polylines throughout the data domain that satisfy $f - c = 0$, where f is the underlying function value and c is the required contour level. The obvious place to begin is on the triangle edges, searching for pairs of vertices (p, q) with $f_p < f_q$ that satisfy $f_p \le c \le f_q$. If the edge length is L the respective distances of the contour crossing points from p and q can be found by simple proportions as $\frac{c - f_p}{f_q - f_p} \cdot L$ and $\frac{f_q - c}{f_q - f_p} \cdot L$. If a contour enters a triangle it must also leave it, so its other two edges are searched similarly. Provided the exit edge does not lie on a boundary the contour can be followed into the next triangle and so on, until either the starting point is found again or the contour leaves the domain. The process is then repeated for all the required contour levels. Figure 6.17 shows this process for the triangulations in Fig. 6.15(a) and Fig. 6.16(c). Note that

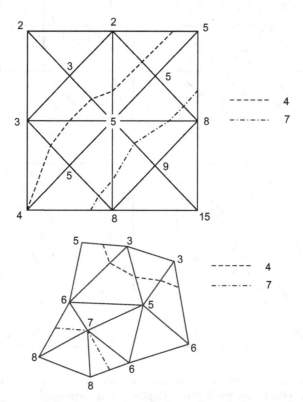

Fig. 6.17. Contour following for triangulations of regularly spaced and scattered data.

dividing a grid cell into four triangles introduces a new vertex into its interior. The data value here can be estimated by first interpolating on the top and bottom cell edges and then on these interpolated points.

The alternative to following a contour is to treat each cell independently, finding all the required contours within it before moving on to the next. We can see the essence of the difference by thinking how we might build a parallelised contourer. One way would be to give each processor node a different cell in which to find all the contours; another would be to give all the cells to all the nodes in order to find one contour each. The larger memory requirement of the latter is balanced by the extra computation requirement of the former, due to the need to "stitch" together all the individual line segments.

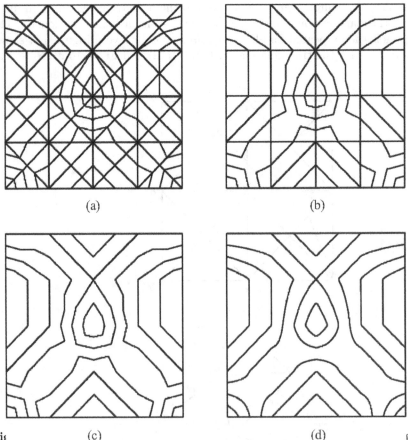

Fig   (c)   (d)   gu-
lation, with (b) and without (c) the original rectangular grid, and (d) using smooth curves within cells. Image credit: IRIS Explorer, test data suite.

When contouring within triangles, the properties described in Sect. 6.2.5 of planes and the lines embedded within them are significant in two ways. Firstly, the straight-line contour segments can be drawn directly between the edge crossings without further computation, making the method quick. Secondly, because this contour segment is embedded within the plane it is guaranteed to represent faithfully the underlying, planar model of the data within the triangle. This in turn ensures that contours cannot cross erroneously. Both are useful properties, but the straight line segments may be rather obvious in the visualization (Fig. 6.18(a)-(c)).

One way to draw curved contours would be to discover the contour-cell edge crossing points and then thread a smooth line between them but, with no guarantee they adhere to an underlying model of the data, these lines now run the risk of crossing one another. A safer alternative is to fit a nonplanar model to each cell that yields a smooth contour line within it (Fig. 6.18(d)).[2] Formulae exist to generate these patches for triangular or rectangular cells; however, the resulting contours may now be too complicated to draw directly, requiring instead to be followed between crossing points. Figure 6.19 shows this process for a rectangular grid cell. It is evident that more evaluations of the underlying function are needed compared to finding just crossing points with the cell edges, resulting in a greater computational overhead.

Before leaving the contour plot it is worth investigating why, when using triangles as the framework, only the arrangement in Fig. 6.15(a) was used for gridded data. Figure 6.20 shows one cell and one contour (level 4.5) of Fig. 6.18(d), which we take as the 'gold standard' for this problem because it

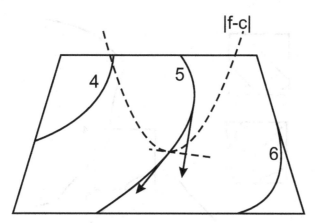

Fig. 6.19. Tracking contours within a cell by minimising $|f - c|$ normal to the current direction of the contour's progress. As well as computing the crossing points with the cell edges, several function evaluations are needed at each small step along the contour.

---

[2] Smoothing contours *across* as well as within the cell boundaries can introduce overshoot errors analogous to those in Fig. 2.21.

represents a contour following a nonplanar approximation to the data. Inset within Fig. 6.20 are the two contour arrangements that would result from the triangulations in Fig. 6.15(b) and (c). Although consisting of line segments, the lower inset reproduces the contour quite well, but the upper one does not. Furthermore, the triangulation that reproduces the contour on the right of the domain will fail to reproduce correctly its mirror on the left. The only triangulation of gridded data that treats both cases equally well is Fig. 6.15(a), which, since it consists of four triangles per cell, involves twice the work of (b) and (c).

To conclude, we have found that even contouring 2D data involves making choices. When using off-the-shelf visualization software, it therefore follows that a degree of detective work may be needed to understand how the representation was produced and to confirm it is valid. When constructing one's own software or application, an apparently insignificant decision at an early stage of the visualization pipeline may lead to an inappropriate representation later on. Problem 6.1 demonstrates what may befall the unwary.

6.2.7 Surface View

Contour plots incorporating a height key can provide quantitative information about the data but have two drawbacks. Firstly, they only show a selection of the data, that is, on the chosen contour levels themselves. Although we can look at the overall visualization and make inferences about data between the levels, if there is rapid variation and widely spaced contours, then detail

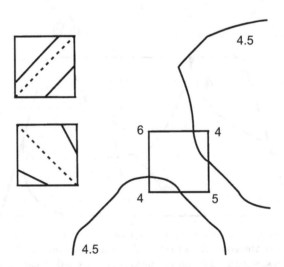

Fig. 6.20. Contouring over two triangles per cell rather than four might seem a tempting way to reduce the work required but can lead to problems if the cell contains a saddle point. A saddle occurs where two opposite vertices have higher values than the chosen contour level and the other two have lower values.

might be missed. Secondly, a contour plot requires a measure of interpretation to understand the highs and lows of the dataset – colour can be a useful aid in addition to a height key. Balanced against these drawbacks is the useful property that contour plots are able to show 2D data within a two-dimensional display. They can therefore be used to visualize a scalar variable over a manifold, such as an aircraft wing, and in other situations we shall meet shortly where the third display dimension already holds some special significance.

If there are no such constraints on the third display dimension, and additionally if the goal of the visualization is to obtain qualitative information about the data, then a surface view is a good technique to consider. A polygonal surface is constructed whose vertices take their x and y coordinates from the values of the independent variables and their z coordinates from the dependent variable values at these points. Figure 6.21 shows the method applied to the triangulations in Fig. 6.15. A similar approach will also serve to generate a surface from the Delaunay triangulation of scattered data that was shown in Fig. 6.16(c).

In fact, Fig. 6.21 is only using part of the information contained in a scalar dataset. Although the z coordinates convey the point values themselves, what is missing is the gradient of the values, that is, the rate at which data changes. We can see this most clearly by thinking again of the contour plot where, as every hill-walker knows, tightly packed lines indicate a steep gradient and wider spacing shows a slower variation in the terrain. Figure 6.22 shows the

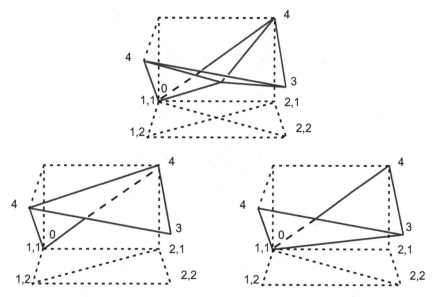

Fig. 6.21. Polygonal surfaces for a single grid cell of the three special triangulations shown in Fig. 6.15.

contours of Fig. 6.18(d) overlaid with arrows to indicate gradients at the data
points.

A surface view can show this type of information – recall the discussion of
Sect. 2.1.1 on shading and highlighting to show the form of an object – but
only if we add normals to the polygons. Surface normals allow for calculating
the amount of light that will be reflected towards the viewer and therefore
how bright each facet will appear. Various schemes are employed for producing
them: they might be calculated on a per-triangle basis in the case of scattered
data, for each of the two- or four-triangle arrangements in Fig. 6.21, or with
one normal standing duty for all the triangles within a single rectangular cell.
This last arrangement fools the eye into believing all the triangles for a cell
lie in one, flat plane. However, as we can see from Fig. 6.21, this will be a
physical impossibility in all but a few cases.

All arrangements that result in one normal per facet will give a faceted
appearance to the visualization. Smooth shading of the surface is possible if
vertex normals are calculated. A common way to do this is to average the
contributions of the normals in the triangles surrounding each point. Figure 6.23 shows four different arrangements for the neighbourhood of a point
for the triangulations we have considered so far. Just as in contouring, the
chosen framework has an influence. Now, different data points are included in
or excluded from the normal calculation because each arrangement produces
a different set of neighbouring triangles. Even interpreting a simple surface

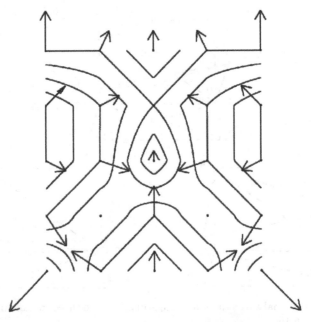

Fig. 6.22. Gradient vectors overlaid on the contours of Fig. 6.18(d). Image credit:
IRIS Explorer, test data suite.

view may therefore involve an unknown commitment: we trust in the results of this calculation to give us an understanding of how rapidly our data varies and yet many visualization packages do not even make its basis clear.

Problem 6.2 is an interesting *trompe l'oeil* that demonstrates the superior power of shading, compared to physical surface displacement, to convey a sense of how data varies.

6.2.8 Height-field Plot

Fairly often we meet data for which a second scalar is defined across the 2D domain. Superimposing surfaces is the 2D analogue of the 1D case of superimposed line graphs but, now that the third display axis is in use, the surface for one scalar will occlude that mapping the other. This violates the uniqueness principle for data-to-attribute mapping. The solution is to use another degree of freedom in the visualization, namely colour, and this technique is known as a height-field plot.

Figure 6.24(a) shows an example where surface height maps to a sine function and surface greyscale to a ramp function. A potential difficulty with this technique is immediately obvious – shading, which we have seen is so important for understanding how the first scalar varies, modifies the greyscale variation that maps the second. The result is that some of the lighter greys (middle to high values) that are in shade appear as dark as the dark grey colour allocated to the lowest data values. Any value-varying colourmap will suffer similarly, and if there are brighter portions caused by specular highlights these will affect a saturation-varying map. Interaction to move the

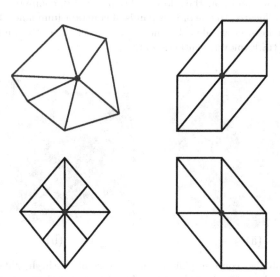

Fig. 6.23. Four different arrangements of neighbourhoods of a single point of scattered and gridded data.

object helps dispel the confusion, as does the availability of colour, but a static image rendered in monochrome may reveal little unless the changes in luminance prior to shading are emphasised. Figure 6.24(b) shows a clearer visualization where the data are allocated to four bands of grey rather than using a continuous variation. Naturally this approach should be applied with care, since improved overall insight has come at the price of understanding the data variation within each band.

Figure 6.24(b) is reminiscent of a shaded contour plot, where the spaces between lines are filled with a single colour or distinctive pattern (Fig. 6.25(a)). This leads to another variant of the technique, which overlays line-based contours on a constant-colour surface (Fig. 6.25(b)).

Shrinking the surface displacement to zero brings us full circle to the realisation that a coloured surface without height is much the same as an image

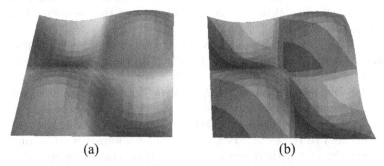

(a)   (b)

Fig. 6.24. In (a), continuous greyscale variation in the presence of shading makes it difficult to understand how the additional scalar varies, compared with (b) where data have been allocated to one of four bands of constant luminance. Shading is still used in (b), but local greyscale coherence helps dispel the confusion evident in (a). Image credit: IRIS Explorer, synthetic data.

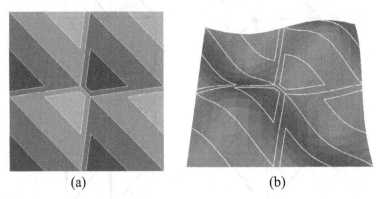

(a)   (b)

Fig. 6.25. A shaded contour plot (a) and a variant of the height-field plot that overlays contour lines for the second variable (b), rather than colour or greyscale. Image credit: IRIS Explorer, synthetic data.

display. However, unlike Fig. 6.12 where data were discontinuous between pixel blocks, now the framework used requires the data to join on at cell edges. This in turn implies some blending between values and its effect on a two-sided step can be seen in Fig. 6.26. Figure 6.26(a) exhibits no interpolation,[3] whilst (b) and (c) interpolate respectively over two and four triangles per grid cell. The two-triangle arrangement is chosen as before with consistently oriented diagonals. In this arrangement the feature aligned north-west to south-east opposes the diagonal orientation whereas its mirror matches it; the two render noticeably differently. The four-triangle arrangement restores the overall symmetry of the image display. Once again, the particular choice of framework has noticeable consequences in the visualization that have nothing at all to do with the data that was input.

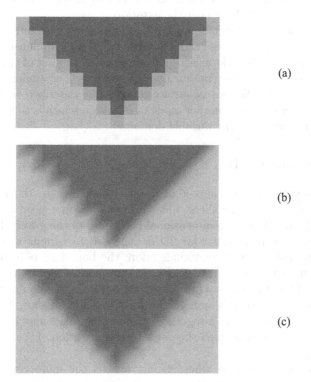

(a)

(b)

(c)

Fig. 6.26. In (a), grey levels are determined as if the data values were constant throughout each rectangular cell. In (b), greyscale is determined according to a planar model of the data over each of two triangles per grid cell. (c) is produced similarly to (b) except it uses four triangles per grid cell. Image credit: IRIS Explorer, synthetic data.

---

[3] Strictly speaking this is nearest neighbour interpolation and it would be more correct to say that (a) exhibits no blending between data values.

6.3 3D Data

With the notable exceptions of the image display and contour plot, all of the single-scalar techniques we have met so far require a visualization whose dimension is greater, by one, than the dimension of the independent variable space. Here then is the conundrum of volume visualization, where the 3D nature of the data domain itself uses up all the available spatial degrees of freedom, before any dependent variable values have even been considered. Even using colour as an additional degree of freedom is not without its difficulties – colouring voxels[4] is all very well, but only data on the outer boundary of the volume can be seen. One of the techniques we shall meet towards the end of this section, volume rendering,[5] therefore employs variable transparency of voxels in order to try to see features on the interior of the volume but without losing sight entirely of those near the exterior.

To understand other techniques for 3D data we can take our cue from the contour plot, which visualizes 2D data within two display dimensions by showing only a selection of it. The selection in this case is a subset of the dependent variable values, that is, the contour lines themselves. The analogue of an isoline for 3D data is called an isosurface and will be described in due course. However, we can consider another mode of selection, which is to visualize over a subset of the independent variable domain.

6.3.1 Reduction to 2D

A simple way to obtain a subset of data with respect to the independent variable domain is to take slices, but to do this we first need a framework. Figure 6.27 shows the three-dimensional analogues of the grid cell and triangular elements we met earlier for 2D data, sliced in various ways. In order to obtain the data needed for visualization, the boundary polygons that result are triangulated and vertex values are interpolated along the original cell edges from the data points. One consideration with this deceptively simple approach is the speed of searching the cells to find the slice. Whilst not a problem for an axial slice of a regular grid, the time taken may become significant for an arbitrarily aligned slice or a tetrahedrisation of scattered points.

A further consideration when slicing data is the more complex shapes that can arise from a body-fitted mesh. As the name implies, a body-fitted mesh is one whose boundary has been constructed so as to follow the outline of some object of interest. A common application is in computational fluid dynamics (CFD), in order to model flow past an obstruction. Figure 6.28(a) shows a mesh constructed around an aerofoil. It originated as a regular grid

---

[4] A voxel is the three-dimensional analogue of a two-dimensional pixel.

[5] *Volume visualization* is the term used for the overall topic of visualizing 3D data, whilst *volume rendering* is a specific technique within this field.

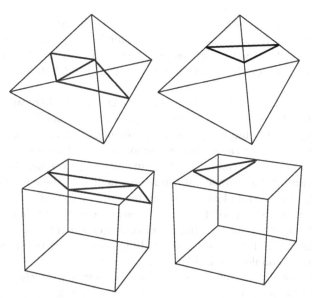

Fig. 6.27. Various slicing operations on tetrahedra and hexahedra. The resulting boundary polygons are then triangulated.

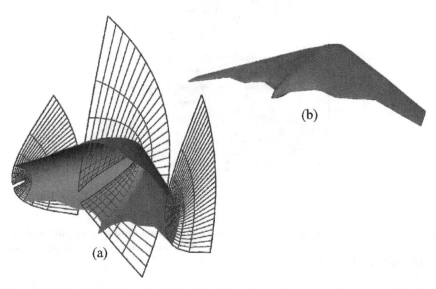

Fig. 6.28. Body-fitted mesh (a) used to investigate flow around an aerofoil. The innermost slice (b) defines the shape of the aerofoil – unlike the slices of Fig. 6.27 it is nonplanar but topologically still constitutes a slice of the domain. Image credit: IRIS Explorer, test data suite.

but has been distorted into the curvilinear one shown. Axial slices of this grid may, in contrast with those of Fig. 6.27, result in nonplanar structures that nonetheless locally are two-dimensional. Figure 6.28(b) shows the shape of the innermost slice of the distorted mesh which, by definition, outlines the aerofoil itself.

Planar or not, the sliced domain is now a 2D manifold (recall Sect. 5.1.2) embedded in 3D space, whose shape and position are therefore significant in their own right. This limits appropriate techniques to the image display or contour plot. Both are theoretically viable visualizations for slices, but the problem with line-based contours is the difficulty of perceiving them correctly within the embedding volume. In the height-field plot the contours overlaid a surface which helped understand their three-dimensional form; without this support the contours' apparent depth may be ambiguous and they may appear to intersect[6] dependent on viewing direction. Interaction to rotate the visualization undoubtedly helps resolve these difficulties, but if this is not feasible another method should be considered first.

An image display within a volume does not suffer from these perceptual problems but having several causes occlusion. Figure 6.29, which we first met in Sect. 2.1.3, demonstrates the problem. Once again, interaction to rotate the object will help and we could also consider animating the slice back and forth.

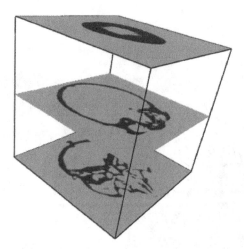

Fig. 6.29. A stack of image plots is a way of visualizing data in a volume, but the more slices are included, the harder it becomes to see their contents. Image credit: IRIS Explorer, test data suite.

---

[6] Contours can only truly intersect at a saddle point.

6.3.2 Isosurface

Obtaining a subset of data with respect to the dependent variable space is a slightly more complex concept than slicing the independent variable domain. We start with the idea of a contour of 2D data which marks the boundary between data of higher value than the chosen level and data of lower value (Fig. 6.30(a)). By definition, all the data values on the contour line are the same and are equal to the chosen level. Extruding this line and the data surrounding it out of the plane of the paper generates a two-dimensional surface (Fig. 6.30(b)). This separates two volumes of data, one above the surface having values higher than the chosen threshold and one below with lower values. On the surface itself all the values equal the threshold, hence this structure is called an isosurface.

In order to generate this surface we return to the mesh over which the data is defined and look again at Fig. 6.27. Although originally demonstrating the generation of slices, we can adapt the idea there to produce polygons that will eventually build up into the isosurface. All that is required is to adjust each polygon's intersections with the cell edges so as to be consistent with the threshold sought, much as we did when finding the crossing points of the contour line with cell edges in the 2D case.

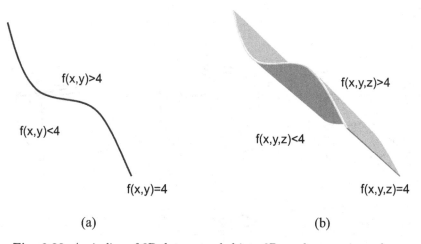

Fig. 6.30. An isoline of 2D data extruded into 3D produces an isosurface.

For gridded data the classical algorithm for doing this is called *marching cubes*. With eight vertices per cell there are $2^8 = 256$ possible ways for the isosurface to pass through. By symmetry this number can be reduced to 15 cases, 14 of which yield portions of the surface comprising 1–4 triangles (Fig. 6.31). The particular configuration of vertices lying above and below the required threshold acts as an index into a table of edge intersections, whose actual locations are then determined according to the vertex values. In order to shade the surface appropriately, the gradient of the data values is found at each cell vertex and these too are interpolated to the intersection positions to provide point normals at the triangle vertices. Calculating surface normals according to the triangle geometry may well be quicker but can produce visual artefacts as demonstrated in Fig. 6.32.

If there are two scalar dependent variables, a useful variant of the technique is to use one variable to define the triangles and the other to colour them. Having found the surface-edge intersections as above using the first set of values, the second set is interpolated to these same positions and a colour mapping is applied. This method is similar in principle to a height-field plot but with an important difference. In a height-field plot the whole domain of the independent variables is visualized, whereas the parts reached by an isosurface are determined by the dependent variable values.

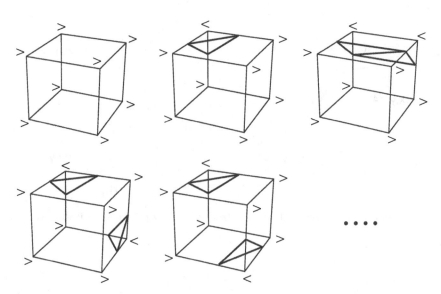

Fig. 6.31. Five of the 15 marching cubes configurations. The symbols > and < respectively indicate the value of a vertex relative to the chosen threshold. Other than for the first case where the surface does not intersect the cell, at least one and at most four separated or connected triangles may be generated.

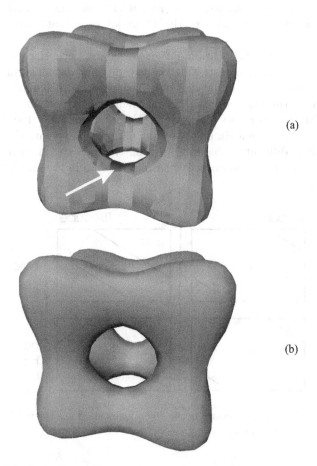

(a)

(b)

Fig. 6.32. Calculating normals according to the surface geometry rather than the data gradients produces artefacts like the one arrowed. The apparent depression in the isosurface in (a) gives a different visual impression of how the data varies compared with (b), even though the triangles generated are the same in the two cases. Image credit: IRIS Explorer, test data suite.

The original marching cubes method could produce holes in surfaces at grid cells that have 'ambiguous faces'. These are like the dilemma presented in Fig. 6.20. A hole will result if two adjacent cube triangulations treat values inconsistently on their shared face (Fig. 6.33); one way of addressing this problem is to define subcases to the 15 major ones that ensure consistent treatment.

Figure 6.34 shows the location of the threshold=7 isosurface for two different tetrahedral cells, demonstrating the two distinct ways a surface can pass through. Gradient information and data for colouring, if required, are found analogously to the gridded case. Having defined this portion of the surface the algorithm moves on to the next tetrahedron, gradually building up the remainder. The apparent simplicity of Fig. 6.34 compared with Fig. 6.31 hides the potentially difficult problem of locating the next cell in an unstructured mesh, which can be accomplished with relative ease in the gridded case.

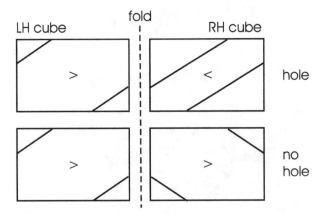

Fig. 6.33. Holes in an isosurface occur when face values are treated inconsistently by adjacent cube triangulations.

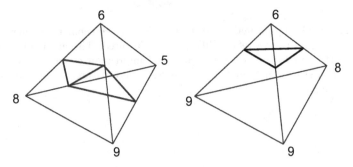

Fig. 6.34. A tetrahedrisation of scattered data yields just three distinct cases, one of which contains no triangles. Finding the next tetrahedron to march to implies the connectivity between cells is known, otherwise all the cells may have to be searched independently and the resulting surface processed to remove duplicate triangle edges.

These methods of isosurface generation provide a cell-by-cell view of the technique, but it is the global properties of the data that govern the nature and extent of the insight that can be gained. Our first observation is that isosurfaces work best for smoothly varying data, otherwise the surface for a single threshold value may comprise many fragments generating little insight. Provided the data is sufficiently smooth, isosurfaces can be of two broad types, each requiring a different approach if we are to get the best out of this technique. Figure 6.30(b) demonstrates an isosurface with open form, the three-dimensional analogue of a contour which enters and leaves the domain via its boundaries. The counterpart of a contour which circles a hilltop in 2D or encloses a valley bottom is an isosurface with closed form, rather like a child's balloon that marks the boundary between low-pressure air outside and the high-pressure air inside. These different forms are significant if we want to draw several isosurfaces at different threshold values. The open form is quite amenable and, provided the individual surfaces are distinguished by means of labels or colour, can generate insight into the overall variation of the dependent variable values (Fig. 6.35).

The closed-form isosurface is another matter – concentric contours in a 2D plot represent little difficulty perceptually but in the 3D case the equivalent is like a 'Russian doll': nested surfaces that have to be peeled away to understand what is inside. Rendering successive thresholds as semi-transparent surfaces can help, but the technique does not scale to several threshold values nearly as easily as its 2D counterpart scales to multiple contour levels. As in Sect. 6.3.1

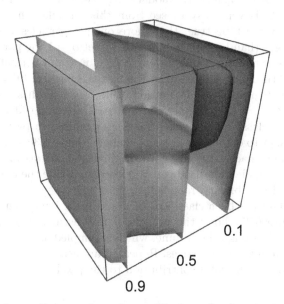

0.1

0.5

0.9

Fig. 6.35. A few well-chosen isosurfaces will show the data variation quite well when they are of open form. Image credit: IRIS Explorer, test data suite.

the problem again is one of occlusion. In visualization the difficult question is not necessarily what to put in but what to leave out. We could use animation as before, not now of the slice position but of the surface's threshold value. In both cases we can think of animation as an extra degree of freedom. Although usually associated with visualizing the independent variable 'time', here it is helping to alleviate visual clutter in a static dataset. Problem 6.4 investigates these alternatives for visualizing several closed-form isosurface thresholds.

6.3.3 Volume Render

In contrast with the previous techniques, volume rendering does not involve subsets but treats the whole domain as a translucent, multicoloured gel. The problem of visualization is not now to make a polygonal representation of the data but to find out the colour and intensity of light travelling towards every part of the two-dimensional view plane. Each small particle of the gel can be considered both to reflect light towards the viewer and to absorb light already on its way that passes through it. This principle is captured for a single particle i by the equation

$$C_{out} = C_{in}(1 - \alpha_i) + C_i \alpha_i \qquad (6.1)$$

where C_{in} and C_{out} respectively denote the light intensity before and after its encounter. The intensity C_i is derived from the particle's assigned colour and shading with its opacity α_i moderating the overall contribution it can make to C_{out}. It is very easy to see from this formula something that we know intuitively must be true, that more opaque particles will reflect and absorb more light than less opaque ones. If we set $\alpha = 1$ the particle becomes opaque, makes maximum contribution to C_{out} in its own right but doesn't let any of C_{in} through. Setting $\alpha = 0$ makes the particle fully transparent, so now it cannot make any contribution of its own regardless of its intrinsic colour; hence $C_{out} = C_{in}$. Colour and opacities are assigned to the data in a process called classification, which may be organised to partition the data into categories, or to emphasise areas of change. Figure 6.36 shows a mapping of greyscale and opacity for the data originally shown as an isosurface in Fig. 6.32. The classification has been organised to divide the data values into three, more-or-less arbitrary, ranges.

Once the data has been classified, (6.1) has to be implemented for all the particles. Figure 6.37 shows the process of ray-casting: rays are fired from each image pixel through the volume, which is sampled at regular intervals by interpolating from the cell vertices. Repeated application of (6.1) composites the samples to give the total contribution to the pixel.

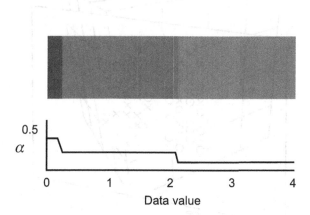

Fig. 6.36. Greyscale classification and corresponding opacity classification of the data of Fig. 6.32, used to produce Fig. 6.39.

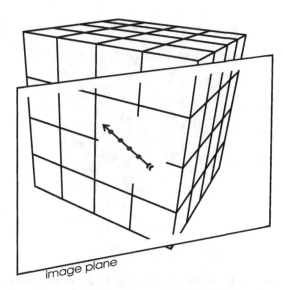

Fig. 6.37. In ray-casting a ray is fired for each image pixel into the volume. Samples along the ray are obtained at equal intervals by interpolation from the data points.

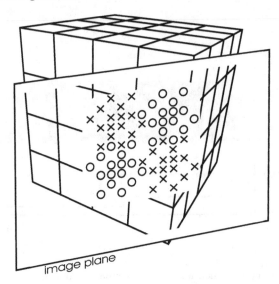

Fig. 6.38. In splatting, footprints are weighted by the voxel values and accumulated into the image.

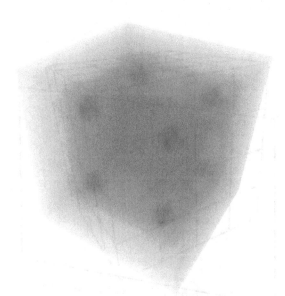

Fig. 6.39. Volume render of the data in Fig. 6.32 using Gaussian (bell-shaped) splats with greyscale classification and opacity classification according to Fig. 6.36. Image credit: IRIS Explorer, test data suite.

Ray-casting is termed an image-order method, since it maps from image to volume. An alternative method, splatting, works from volume to image. It views the volume as a set of overlapping but nonetheless individual contributions positioned at voxel locations. The projection of each contribution to the image, called a footprint, determines the image portion that is affected by that voxel. The different contributions are then accumulated for each pixel within the footprint. Figure 6.38 illustrates the process and Fig. 6.39 shows the result, using the classification in Fig. 6.36. Splatting was developed to make volume rendering possible at interactive rates, though hardware and software developments mean that the performance gap between the two methods is closing.

Problems

6.1. Run the provided software demonstrating contouring of gridded data over triangular and rectangular meshes. What methods were used (consider both the framework and the model fitted to the data) to produce the upper, middle, and lower contour plots? To what extent would each be regarded as a correct depiction of the data?

6.2. Run the provided software demonstrating the use of normal information to generate shading on a surface view. Rotate the object, which shows one peak and one trough, back and forth through a moderate angle to understand its form. Now rotate it through a larger angle – do you notice anything odd about this surface view? Switch on the second surface. What do you notice about this new object, compared with the first?

6.3. Run the provided software comparing isosurfaces and volume rendering. What three isosurface threshold values do you think correspond most closely with the features that are picked out in green, yellow and orange by the volume render technique?

6.4. Run the provided software comparing semi-transparent isosurfaces with an animation of different threshold values. Set the isosurface values you found for Prob. 6.3 and adjust transparency so you can see all three surfaces. Does this visualization remind you of another technique for visualizing volumes?

Now compare this visualization with an animation that shows all the threshold values in between. You may need to watch it several times to obtain a good overall impression. Where would you use the static technique and where the animated one?

7

Visualizing Vectors

Vectors are another type of dependent variable commonly encountered in visualization, and they afford a variety of interpretations. They may, for instance, describe the deformation a beam undergoes as a load is applied, or the rate of change over time of the concentration of a chemical in a reaction. However, the most common application by far is to understand flow, often the output of computational fluid dynamics (CFD) calculations, but also encompassing electromagnetic, as opposed to velocity, fields. This chapter will especially concentrate on this area, and in particular the case of steady, or stationary, flow. Visualization of unsteady flow is a specialist area beyond the scope of an introductory book – some pointers to further sources are given in Chap. 8.

Regardless of the application, all vectors are characterised by having a magnitude (a scalar quantity) and a direction defined according to some coordinate system. Vector data that is output from a simulation is therefore commonly described in terms of its individual components along each of the system's axes. As well as the familiar Cartesian system, which is typically the one supported by most visualization systems, in Sect. 5.1.2 we saw polar coordinate systems for 2D and 3D. These latter two are quite commonly used in simulation, so often the first step to visualization is therefore a conversion between the two, in order to obtain data in a form the system can handle. For scalar dependent variables this will involve converting how the data locations are held (recall that positions are vectors too), whilst for vector dependent variables it will additionally entail converting the different vector components.

In scalar visualization the display dimension was generally found to be one greater that the independent variable dimension, so a natural order in which to approach the techniques in Chap. 6 was according to the dimension of the data domain. For vector data the situation is different, with the display dimension governed instead by the number of vector components. The sections within this chapter thus follow a repeating pattern, with visualizations of two-dimensional vectors preceding three-dimensional ones. Overall the approach is to deal first with point-based direct visualizations of flow since in principle these need no interpolation and therefore no underlying framework. These are followed by techniques that construct geometric objects to give a sparse representation of the flow and lastly flow textures, which provide a dense representation. The chapter closes with some cautionary remarks regarding unsteady flow.

7.1 Arrow Plot

An obvious and intuitive visualization of vector data is to draw arrows – the arrow length can signify the magnitude of the velocity whilst its direction helps understand the relative sizes of the different components. In its simplest form an arrow is placed with its base at each of the data points, so no interpolation is required, and an overall impression is given of the flow. Figure 7.1(a) shows this technique applied to the electromagnetic field around two dipoles. Figure 7.1(b) shows an alternative, a hedgehog, which dispenses with the arrow head in order to reduce cluttering of the visualization. In this case the vector's direction may be coded by fading the line from its base to its head.

Even such a simple visualization of two-dimensional vectors entails some risks and possibly some trade-offs of insight versus accuracy. For instance, it is common to apply a scaling factor to the magnitudes in order to generate optimum length arrows, that is, accommodating the largest magnitudes in the dataset but still allowing us to see the smallest. This latter requirement may still produce arrows for the largest-magnitude vectors whose heads approach their neighbours' bases, as in some parts of Fig. 7.1. The overall effect can divert visual interest along the vector direction, moving it away from the data positions that are genuinely associated with these large values. One solution may be to use arrows of equal length but whose widths indicate vector magnitude, whilst another places identical arrows but colours them according to magnitude. Distributing arrows differently across the domain is yet another possible approach: subsampling a regular grid is generally easy but may mask rapid variations in the data; resampling onto scattered points can solve perceptual problems arising from the regularity of the data grid but will involve interpolation of the original data values. These variants require some care in their application since subsampled or resampled points may depict a different range of data to the original values, both in terms of the independent variable values and the dependent variables. In general, bounding boxes and data ranges applying to colour maps should reflect the whole dataset, even when they are employed to visualize a subset.

When the vectors are three-dimensional, additional considerations come into play. Arrows drawn as lines can be difficult to perceive, due to the lack of depth cues: a short arrow apparently upright in the image may in fact be a long horizontal arrow foreshortened by perspective. Interaction to rotate the scene will help as we have seen before, as will the construction of solid arrows since shading helps convey orientation. Solid arrows also carry colour information more readily than lines, due to their greater surface area, though

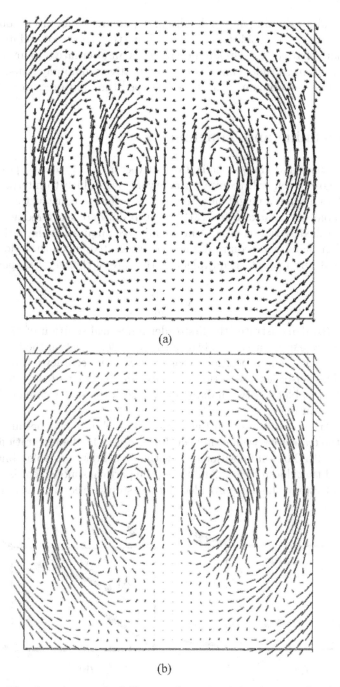

(a)

(b)

Fig. 7.1. The electromagnetic field around a pair of dipoles, visualized (a) using line arrows and (b) using lines with no arrowhead. Image credit: IRIS Explorer, test data suite.

the potential for shading and highlighting apparently to modify colour (recall Sect. 6.2.8) must be considered. Before we leave the arrow plot and its variants we also note that colour, already described as an alternative to arrow length for conveying magnitude, can of course alternatively map any scalar variable defined across the domain such as fluid temperature and pressure.

7.2 Streamline and Timeline

Just as in the scalar case, visualizations of vector data involving positions in between those given will require a framework over which to interpolate. For regular data a point's neighbours are used as before to construct a quadrilateral (2D domain) or hexahedral (3D) mesh. If data are scattered a triangulation or tetrahedrisation is used. Additionally, techniques that have their roots in particle tracing will require data to be integrated, since the velocity $\mathbf{v}$ of particle p at any instant is equivalent to the rate of change of its position $\mathbf{p}$, i.e.,

$$\mathbf{v} = \frac{d\mathbf{p}}{dt} \tag{7.1}$$

Figure 7.2(b) demonstrates the first-order numerical solution of (7.1), where tiny timesteps Δt are used to advance the particle, based on the interpolated velocity at each previous position. In practice greater accuracy usually requires the use of higher-order integration schemes. The accuracy of the interpolation scheme used to blend between data values (recall the scalar case of Fig. 6.26) may also be an issue.

In fact, the particle path in Fig. 7.2 should look familiar, because it is the same as the trajectory we met in Sect. 5.1.3, Fig. 5.4. The integration of (7.1) has produced 1D ordinal position data with independent variable 'time' from a vector field that doesn't vary. Animating the particle's movement is a natural way to understand the flow, provided the timesteps are equal. The potential to

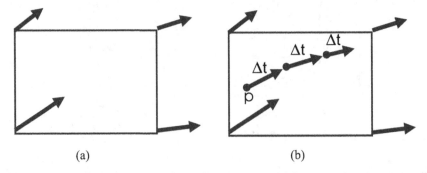

(a)   (b)

Fig. 7.2. Point-based direct visualization with arrows (a) requires no interpolation of data values. Tracing the route (b) of particle p, on the other hand, requires both interpolation and integration of the velocity field.

attribute this animation wrongly to a time variation of the underlying vectors is, however, obvious and is why such fields are referred to as 'steady', or 'stationary'. The 'steady' adjective supports the idea that time progresses and particles move, but they are transported through a flow which is unchanging in its form.

In a steady flow, the particle follows a streamline of the velocity field which is everywhere tangential to it. Figure 7.3 demonstrates this idea, with a 2D flow that simply goes round in circles at constant speed throughout the domain.

As suggested above, magnitude (the speed of the flow) and direction (in this case, does it flow clockwise or anticlockwise) can be conveyed by animating particles along the streamline. If animation is not available, then, since magnitude is a scalar quantity, the streamline may be coloured to indicate speed. If colour has already been used to indicate some scalar other than speed, alternatively a snapshot of several particles at different instants will convey speed via their spacing. Indicating the start of the streamline as the seeding position allows the flow direction to be inferred (Fig. 7.4).

Another way of representing flow with lines is to join a set of particles released at the same time. Figure 7.5(a) shows four streamlines of the vector field in Fig. 7.3(a). In Fig. 7.5(b) are the timelines formed by connecting the seed points of these streamlines and taking snapshots as they follow the paths. Timelines are familiar from the athletics track (Fig. 7.5(c)) as the curved

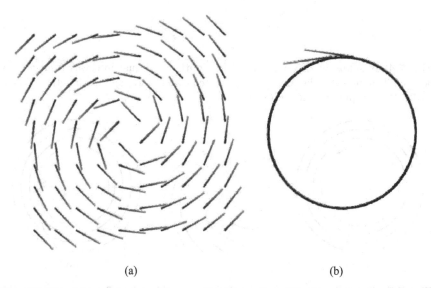

(a)   (b)

Fig. 7.3. A velocity field (a) with one of its streamlines (b). The streamline is everywhere tangential to the flow: vectors lying along it (just two are shown) represent the instantaneous directions of a particle as it follows this path. Image credit: IRIS Explorer, test data suite.

starting positions s that ensure all runners cover an equal distance during the race. If everyone were to run at the same speed, as in this example, they would all cross the finish f at the same time.

7.3 Streamribbon, Streamsurface, and Streamtube

Streamlines transfer in theory to three-dimensional vectors but, just as for line arrows, there are perceptual difficulties due to a lack of depth information. One solution is to render the streamline as geometry that can be shaded to produce the necessary cues – Fig. 7.6 compares a line-drawn streamline through a 3D domain with one drawn as an extruded circle. Many polygonal streamlines might, however, be costly to render or cause occlusion; hence

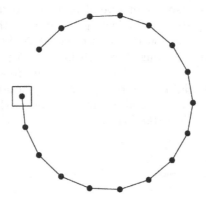

Fig. 7.4. A snapshot of several particles emitted at equal intervals from a seed position demonstrates the speed of the flow (constant, here) and its direction. Image credit: IRIS Explorer, test data suite.

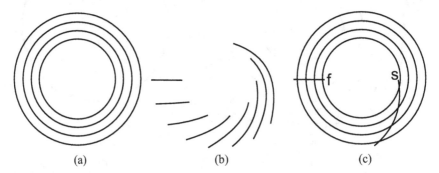

(a)   (b)   (c)

Fig. 7.5. Streamlines (a) of the circular vector field in Fig. 7.3 and timelines (b) formed by joining particles released into this flow at the same time and following their progress. If speeds are constant, each timeline cuts off the same distance (c) measured along each streamline.

illuminated streamlines were developed to address these problems. They employ line segments but use the texture mapping hardware of modern graphics workstations to generate shading and partial transparency at interactive rates.

Other approaches based on streamlines also draw extended objects, not just for perceptual reasons but specifically to examine some particular characteristic of the flow. Streamribbons can be useful for understanding rotation in flow. They may be constructed either by tiling the space between two adjacent streamlines or by extruding a line along a single streamline to define a narrow two-dimensional strip. The orientation of the line is controlled by the vorticity of the flow (Fig. 7.7).

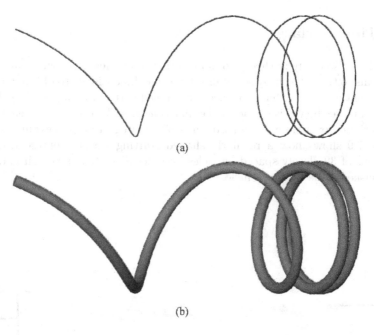

(a)

(b)

Fig. 7.6. Streamlines passing through a 3D domain drawn (a) simply as lines. Depth is hard to perceive and the line appears to intersect itself, which it cannot do if it is always tangential to the vector field. The same streamline drawn as a polygonal tube (b) can be rendered with shading and hidden surface removal. Image credit: IRIS Explorer, test data suite.

A streamsurface which, like a streamline, is everywhere tangential to the flow, extends this idea further. It may be constructed by tiling the space between adjacent streamlines or be calculated directly from the flow itself. Figure 7.8(b) shows a streamsurface calculated from the streamlines in Fig. 7.8(a). Note how the three-dimensional flow is quite difficult to understand from the streamlines, but lighting and shading of the streamsurface reveals a noticeable bulge around the vehicle. A variant of this technique restores the sense of flow direction by cutting out arrow shapes (stream arrows) from the streamsurface.

If the line of seed positions forms a closed loop the streamsurface bends round to form a streamtube. Note however that this is not necessarily equivalent to the polygonal tube of Fig. 7.6, which was generated by sweeping a circle along a single streamline, much as the ribbon of Fig. 7.7 was created by sweeping a line along whilst rotating it. Polygons swept along a streamline (sometimes called stream polygons) can help to visualize quantities derived from the flow at points along the streamline. A simple case would be to sweep a circle whose radius showed flow speed, but the surface generated might not be tangential to the flow, as it must be in the case of a streamtube.

7.4 Time Surface

Timelines also apply in theory to more vector components but with analogous problems to those faced by streamlines in three dimensions. To obtain a useful variant of timelines we have to place several seed particles on a (usually) planar surface and see how this surface moves in the flow. As before, this is steady flow and variation over time is a consequence of the integration process in Fig. 7.2. Figure 7.9 shows how a regularly shaped starting surface representing the positions of 32 closely spaced particles becomes distorted as the air carrying it is pushed aside by the vehicle.

Fig. 7.7. A streamribbon demonstrates flow rotation by extruding a line along a streamline. Image credit: IRIS Explorer, synthetic data.

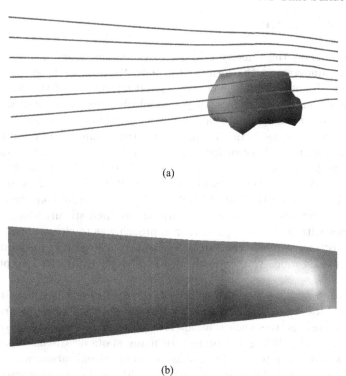

(a)

(b)

Fig. 7.8. A streamsurface can be constructed from several streamlines and, since it can be lit and shaded, helps to understand how the flow moves towards the viewer in the vicinity of the vehicle. Image credit: IRIS Explorer, test data suite.

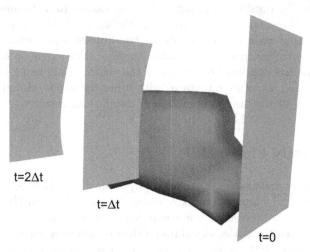

t=2Δt

t=Δt

t=0

Fig. 7.9. A planar and rectangular surface remains planar as time progresses but its right-hand edge is distorted inwards in the vicinity of the vehicle.

7.5 Flow Texture

Arrow plots show the velocity field across the whole domain, but it may be difficult to understand the form of the flow. Techniques based on particle tracing, on the other hand, may give a good impression of the flow but are highly dependent on choosing seed points which generate interesting streamlines. Flow textures try to give a dense representation of the flow which also conveys a sense of its form. In appearance the technique is reminiscent of paint in a container whose surface has been flecked with a contrasting colour. Stirring the paint with a narrow blade spreads the flecks in the direction of the flow, leaving a lasting imprint. Figure 7.10(b) shows a flow texture of the velocity field in Fig. 7.10(a) produced by line integral convolution. This method of calculation spreads a texture out mathematically along multiple streamlines within the flow. An earlier approach was to elongate spots in the vector direction, whilst recent approaches have utilised texture hardware in graphics workstations to render blended noise images distorted according to the flow.

Extension of these types of technique to three dimensions runs into two main difficulties. Firstly, until recently the computation time required, even in two dimensions, was such that in three dimensions it would become prohibitive. Secondly, filling a volume with many spots or streaks representing the flow would generate a problem akin to volume visualization, which is itself a major undertaking. These issues are being addressed by current research but in off-the-shelf software it is still common to find flow texture techniques essentially limited to two-dimensional situations. Visualization of a 2D domain as a two-dimensional manifold within three-dimensional space may be catered for, or it may be possible to apply a 2D flow texture to a streamsurface object. Beyond these, some care is required: slicing a 3D domain and applying a technique that is only appropriate to two-dimensional vectors effectively ignores the vector components normal to the slice. The extent to which this is an approximation depends very much on the velocity field being analysed. In these situations, use of flow textures with other techniques described in this chapter may give the best combination of insight and veracity.

7.6 Unsteady Flow

In steady flows the trajectory followed by a single particle is the same as a streamline, and many particles released successively from the same seed position will spread out along one streamline as in Fig. 7.4. In unsteady flows we can still draw the trajectory through the domain of a particle released at a particular time, but the flow it experiences towards the end of its travel is not the same as it was at the beginning. Another particle released a short time after it will not therefore follow the same path. Joining up several such particles with a line now generates not a streamline, but a streakline. The

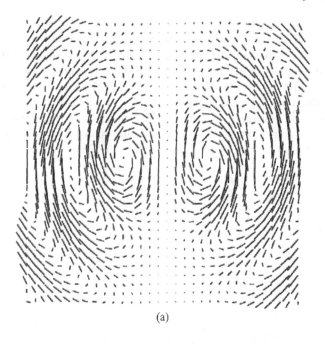

(a)

(b)

Fig. 7.10. Flow texture (b) generated by line integral convolution of the velocity field in (a). The texture emphasises streamlines in the velocity field but without the need to choose seed points. Image credit: IRIS Explorer, test data suite.

concept of a streamline is still valid but only for a snapshot of the flow, as if it were frozen at some instant in time. Animating the development of a streakline can be a useful way to understand an unsteady flow but it should be noted that animating a sequence of instantaneous streamlines is not equivalent. The latter neglects development between timesteps, in much the same way as a slice that neglects orthogonal vector components treats three-dimensional vectors as if they were two-dimensional. A number of the most promising developments to date for visualizing unsteady flows are in the area of flow texture synthesis and some pointers to further reading are given in Chap. 8.

Problems

7.1. Run the provided software demonstrating the effect of interpolation when generating streamlines. First adjust the pitch of the spiral in order to understand the rôle of the parameter α. Now change the interpolation scheme and then adjust the height at which the seed particle is released. What do you observe and what is the likely explanation?

7.2. Run the provided software demonstrating flow within a double glazing panel. Identify the two techniques in use and describe why this visualization is an approximation. How significant is the approximation in this case?

8

Bibliography and Further Reading

Introduction

A fascinating survey of pre-computer visualization is given by Collins [15]. He concludes that, whilst there is little in computer-generated visualization that is new in terms of techniques, computers do nonetheless make visualization a possibility for large quantities of data. Some useful insights into the factors contributing to the rapid development of computer visualization in the late 1980s are given by Brodlie in [3].

The National Science Foundation report edited by McCormick, DeFanti and Brown that so concentrated minds and effort can be found at [38]. This report gave us the famous "'fire hoses' of data" quote that has become the mantra of scientific visualization.

Potential and Pitfalls

A comprehensive but approachable book on how we perceive space, objects, movement, and colour is by Gregory [21]. On discussing animation I have substituted the term 'beta movement', where Gregory uses 'phi phenomenon', on the basis of Wikipedia's article [64] and associated links. A complementary reference to Gregory on our perception of the three-dimensional form of objects is by Haber [23], who also gives an account but with special consideration of the requirements for visualizing scientific data.

Gregory's book is home to a whole host of further reading about vision, including a reference to Grimes's work [22] on hiding scene changes during the eye movements we call saccades. The increasingly outrageous changes in images that Grimes was able to pass by his subjects without them noticing makes for interesting reading and leaves us wondering just what 'sleight of eye' may be possible in this age of digital image enhancement.

All of Edward Tufte's exquisite books are a must-read for anyone aiming to present data visually. I found his *Visual Display of Quantitative Information*

[55] especially helpful on 'graphical integrity', one aspect of which is the misuse of chart perspective described in this chapter. Note, however, that Tufte eschews pie charts, even flat ones!

Brodlie [1] (pp 38–39) characterises the filter process of the dataflow visualization model as one which attempts to reconstruct what is underlying the data. The importance of what underlies the data, but now with an emphasis on controlling interpolation, is also the topic of Brodlie and Mashwama [7]. As well as putting forward the mathematics of the subject for 1D, 2D, and 3D data, they include some surface views that show analogous behaviour to the line graphs of Fig. 2.21. Satisfying bounds is also the subject of Brodlie et al. [4] but here data values in between those given are interpolated by a summation of basis functions defined across the whole domain, rather than piecewise within the cells of a mesh joining the points.

Models and Software

Wright [68] and others have described computational steering as an extension of the standard dataflow pipeline. Following the NSF report [38] there was a good deal of work to realise computational steering, with papers appearing in the literature that covered both systems developments and applications of steering (see, for example, [8, 30, 37, 60]). In a sense, computational steering was a solution waiting for a problem; a criticism commonly levelled at it was the small number of interesting simulations that could be tackled in real time. With the advent of grid computing (see, for example, [19]) computational steering has experienced an upsurge of interest (see, for example, [5, 44]). Grid computing, with its greater access to computational resources, offers the prospect of studying a much wider range of more complex problems than was hitherto possible. Much of the work in the UK takes place under the umbrella of the Research Councils' e-Science programme and proceedings of the e-Science 'All Hands' meetings are published annually. Their web sites are noted in the Appendix.

Wood's PhD thesis [67] investigates a number of different approaches to collaborative visualization and client–server visualization, dealing with the issues that were raised in Sect. 3.2.2. Before doing so he first gives a thoroughly lucid summary of the various models of visualization that were developed in the late 1980s and 1990s. He also demonstrates very clearly the relationship between the Haber and McNabb [25] and Upson et al. [56] approaches to constructing a dataflow model for visualization. An excellent report on the state-of-the-art in distance and collaborative visualization is given by Brodlie et al. [6].

The framework for describing visualization software that is presented in this chapter is a combination of the approach put forward by Gallop [20] and Brodlie [3]. Upson et al. describe very clearly the drivers leading to their development of AVS in [56]. A summary of what constitutes an MVE and descriptions of the five original MVEs described in Sect. 3.3 are given in [13]. For readers wanting comprehensive descriptions of current software there are chapters on amira, AVS/Express, IRIS Explorer, ParaView, SCIRun and VTK, amongst others, in [26]. These chapters and the URLs noted in the Appendix for each of the organisations or software products mentioned were the major source of information in compiling the section on software. IRIS Explorer, the particular visualization software used to produce the screenshots in this book, is described by Walton [61].

Colour in Scientific Visualization

Once again, Gregory [21] gives an extremely readable account of how we perceive colour, including a flavour of some of the historical debate that surrounded this field. Hearn and Baker's book on computer graphics [27] also includes a very useful chapter (Chapter 12) on colour with its main focus on colour models. They also cover the HLS model (hue, lightness, and saturation), which is not included in this book but may often be found in software packages as well as or in place of an HSV representation. Haber [23] has some useful insights on the nonlinearity of colour perception and its consequences for scientific visualization.

A number of interesting points made by Gregory [21] compare vision with some of the other senses. One relates to the perception of a single colour as a mixture of responses by different receptors and emphasises how fundamentally different this is to our separate perception of sounds of multiple frequencies. Thus in a chord of music we will hear the differently pitched notes quite separately whereas in colour the different cone cell responses combine to produce one sensation. Another remark deals with the frequency of the stimulus. For light, sensing the very high frequencies involved requires a system of chemical intermediaries, the cone cell photopsins. Contrast this with our sense of touch, where textures are perceived by the stimulation of skin mechanoreceptors that are directly connected to nerve fibres. One consequence is that in computer systems, visual refresh rates can be rather lower than those needed for haptic display.

In the discussion of colour perception I have used the terms short-, medium-, and long-wavelength receptor (see, for example, [65]) as well as the terms blue, green, and red cone cells, since both are in common usage in reference material. The peak cone sensitivity values used to draw Fig. 4.2 are from [65].

There is a great deal of material available on the subject of colour vision deficiency; unfortunately not all of it is completely consistent in its use of terminology. The prefixes prot-, deuter-, and trit- are invariably used to refer to the long-, medium-, and short-wavelength ('red', 'green', and 'blue') systems respectively but usage of the suffixes -anope (the person), and -anopia and -anomaly (the degree of deficiency) varies. Thus, some will apply the term 'protanope' only to someone with protanopia (implying an extreme form) whilst for others it will include someone with protanomaly. Yet others use only '-anopia' forms rather than making a distinction by means of '-anomaly' forms. This can be confusing for someone venturing for the first time into the material. However, Gregory [21] and others clarify by describing extreme forms of colour vision deficiency as those where only two primaries are needed to match the range of seen colours, and less extreme forms as needing three primaries but in different proportions to the usual.[1] Given the subtle differences to be seen in various descriptions in the literature, these fundamental principles may be more helpful in understanding sources than attempting a strict distillation of terms.

The idea of colour vision deficiency as a lower-dimensional gamut also occurs in Rasche et al. [49], where a process for re-colouring images is described not only with these viewers in mind but also for publication in greyscale. Their work concentrates on preserving both colour *and* luminance differences and will be particularly helpful when conveying luminance-balanced images in greyscale, since the usual translation based only on Y will of course result in no detail being captured.

I do not have a colour vision deficiency, but I know a number of people who do. In trying to understand their experiences it has been worthwhile looking at various internet sites that convert images to use a reduced palette of colours. The address of one site, Vischeck, is noted in the Appendix and includes links to a number of others. When viewing any such images, though, bear in mind the caveats in Sect. 4.2 and resist attempting a simple 'translation' to apparent colour equivalents.

In the section demonstrating the effect of colour on perceived brightness, the idea of showing the locus of constant $R + G + B$ as a plane perpendicular to the line of greys is due to Bunks' Figure 5.5 [11], from which it follows naturally to represent constant luminance as a tilted plane. Our respective graphical comparisons of the RGB and HSV colour models were achieved independently but it is gratifying to see their similarity. The coefficients I use for the luminance calculation are described by Poynton [47].

My line drawings of the inverted cone for the HSV model do not reproduce Smith's hexcone [51] since for simplicity I have taken the hue disk to be circular. There should be no loss of generality, however, since the depiction of the axes in these figures is conceptual, that is, the geometry of the solid is not used to calculate the value or saturation of any actual colours. The screenshots and software, on the other hand, do show the origin of the hexcone in the six-sided saturation surface and the orthographic projection of the value surface.

Figure 4.14, which shows a distorted RGB cube standing on its black vertex, was derived by judging very approximately the relative differences of various-hued colour maps on my own computer monitor. Since generating

---

[1] The term 'dichromacy' may also be seen for needing two primaries and 'anomalous trichromacy' for needing unusual amounts of three primaries.

this figure I have become aware of other representations of three-dimensional gamut solids (see, for example, [29, 39, 50]) that are similar in appearance but undoubtedly better founded. The colour spaces mentioned in these sources are an initiative of the Commission Internationale de l'Eclairage (CIE) to develop descriptions of colour that exhibit better perceptual uniformity than those based on RGB, HSV, and other similar models. As mentioned in Sect. 4.4, colour mapping in a perceptually uniform space would make the specification of linear colour maps much easier since, by definition, such spaces aim to make equal distances result in equally noticeable changes in the colour that is seen. As well as demonstrating gamut mapping the last reference in this list also plots a yellow-blue colour map within a perceptually uniform space according to the device's RGB coordinates. Remarkably, the sequence points that are regularly spaced in RGB exhibit roughly a 3:1 variation in length when measured in perceptual units. This brings home a point that must be understood very clearly, which is that the strategies put forward in Sect. 4.4.3 can only go some way towards compensating for the perceptual shortcomings of RGB and HSV. Until software adopts colour specification in terms of uniform spaces expressed for the device in question, we have to accept that truly reproducible and linear colour mapping for visualization is an unattainable goal.

Choosing Techniques

In describing data systematically I have followed the recommendations made by Gallop [20], separating the independent and dependent variables first and avoiding rolling their dimensions together. Thus, for example, in this book a contour plot and a surface view are both described as techniques for 2D scalar data or, occasionally, "2D techniques." Some sources, however, will call the latter a "3D technique," not because it can handle 3D data but because it requires three display dimensions to draw it. Likewise a 2D bar chart, the name given by Brodlie [1] to a technique for 2D nominal scalar data, is used in preference to "3D bar chart," which is how it will sometimes be described elsewhere. The convention used thus tries to avoid confusion by having numerical dimension labels reflect only the properties of the data domain, whether or not they are describing the data or the technique visualizing that data. This enumeration may differ from the degrees of freedom required for visualization, which in turn comprise the display dimensions in use (equivalent to the spatial dimensions of the AVO), plus colour and possibly animation (AVO attributes). To further underline the distinction, the number of degrees of freedom are always written literally.

Underpinning this approach is a heavy dependence on thinking about data in the abstract, rather than via its visualization, a point that is stressed throughout this chapter. This is accomplished by classifying data as an independent variable space with dependent variable space(s) attached at each point, ideas that draw on the mathematical theory of fibre bundles as put forward by Butler and Pendley [10]. Fibre bundles are further described and are used as a basis for a visualization data model by Haber et al. [24]. The two parts of [24] thus relate back to the two scenarios of Fig. 5.1: fibre bundles are particularly useful when considering the mathematical model of a problem whereas its numerical solution produces discrete data that must be accommodated in a data model if we are to visualize it.

Once the data has been classified, adopting a taxonomic approach to choosing techniques owes much to Brodlie [1], but with the inclusion of trajectories suggested by the canonical graphic representations in Butler and Pendley [10], Table 1. Dispensing with the 'point' type in [1] in favour of a description as 1D nominal vector data is consistent with later refinements proposed by Brodlie [2] to enable greater separation between the data and the means of viewing that data. Scatterplots are thus seen as near relatives of trajectories (1D ordinal data), but with a display that is reduced to points due to nominal data having no inherent order. Unlike [1] and [2], however, I do not attempt any formalism other than to introduce the concept of manifolds instead of the notion of a restriction operator for data and views.

Visualizing Scalars

Modelling data over triangles and tetrahedra underpins much of visualization. Nielson's survey [41] compares a number of algorithms for triangulation and tetrahedrisation and describes a variety of interpolants constructed to fulfill different aims. As well as providing a comprehensive treatise in itself, this work also includes a bibliography of more than 250 further sources.

The broad division of contour methods into those that follow isolines and those that treat each cell in turn is described by Snyder [52], though the driving factors then (1978) were not memory versus computation resource but memory versus plotter pen travel. When re-reading the literature of the time it is interesting to observe how distant we have become from the computer hardware in the intervening years.

Powell and Sabin [46] note the value of contouring a function with C^1 continuity in order to generate isolines with direction continuity, compared with the ad hoc approach of threading a smooth curve through the crossings of the contour lines with the cell edges. However, their ultimate aim is to use a parametric form to follow the contour of a piecewise quadratic approximation over triangular elements, rather than to track contours by progressive approximation. Preusser [48] describes finding zeros of $f - c$ (Fig. 6.19) by searching with regula falsi normal to the curve of the contour. Contours are generated in topological sequence on a cell-by-cell basis and the method is generally applicable to nonlinear interpolants within linearly bounded domains. The particular focus of [48] is bicubic interpolation within rectangular cells, whereas Fig. 6.18(d) is equivalent to tracking the bilinear interpolant (C^0 continuous);

hence contours are not smooth across cell edges. The potential for the bicubic interpolant to exceed bounds is discussed by Brodlie and Mashwama [7], who demonstrate the visual effect using surface views.

Snyder [52], Cottafava and Le Moli [16], and Crane [17] all describe connecting contour intersections on rectangular cell edges with straight lines. Each algorithm results in a different strategy for resolving the ambiguity caused by having an intersection on each cell side, which is how the dilemma of Fig. 6.20 is more usually presented. Brodlie [2] points out that joining intersections with straight lines when the interpolant is bilinear is itself an approximation, even for cases with no ambiguity, and affirms the approach of dividing each cell into four triangles as a means of resolution (cf. Fig. 6.18(a) to (c)).

On the value of gradient information in understanding data, Haber and McNabb [25] describe a surface view constructed of polygons whose vertex z coordinates are a nonlinear function of the data values and whose vertex normals are directly defined by the data gradients. This decoupling of the physical surface generation from the normal generation was the inspiration for the demonstration of shading comprising Prob. 6.2. However, in the latter the normals are generated from the geometry that would have been produced by the surface displacement, rather than directly from the data.

A useful review of recent advances in volume visualization is given by Brodlie and Wood [9]. This paper also establishes the framework that is applied here and clarifies terminology. A good reference for readers aiming to begin research or development in this field is Chen et al. [14].

Marching cubes is described in Lorensen and Cline's seminal paper [36]. Wilhelms and Van Gelder [66] and Nielson and Hamann [42] each identify 'ambiguous faces' created by the approach in [36] as potentially leading to 'holes' in the isosurface. Both aim to fix the problem by defining subcases, though in different ways. These references deal with the topological correctness of the resulting surface; other work to improve the robustness and accuracy of the method is surveyed in [9].

The treatment of a volume as a composition of particles, each of which reflect and absorb light, follows the description by Mueller et al. [40]. Equation (6.1) is sample compositing in back-to-front order as described by Levoy [33], but dropping the λ suffix for simplicity as suggested by Brodlie and Wood [9]. Front-to-back compositing and the potential it brings for early ray termination in volume rendering is one of the efficiency improvements to ray-casting discussed by Levoy [34]. The splatting algorithm was proposed by Westover [63] to improve efficiency of volume rendering over ray-casting approaches. As Mueller et al. observe [40], its advantages accrue from the potential to precompute the footprints and the effective restriction of interpolations to 2D, compared with the more expensive 3D reconstruction of ray-casting.

Visualizing Vectors

Good overviews of flow visualization in general are by Post and van Wijk [45] and by Weiskopf and Erlebacher [62]. Both also include sections on feature-based visualization, which is not covered in this book. A classification of approaches to flow visualization, which is broadly that followed here, is given by Laramee et al. [32], who then go on to survey the state-of-the-art for texture-based techniques. The visualization of unsteady flow is the particular topic of Lane [31]. Another comprehensive survey of unsteady flow literature is given by Liu and Moorhead [35] before going on to describe their method for acceleration of line integral convolution for unsteady flows.

On the topic of flow visualization using geometric objects, Zöckler et al. [69] describe the generation of illuminated streamlines, whilst parametric stream-surfaces and implicit streamsurfaces are respectively described by Hultquist [28] and van Wijk [58]. An evaluation of two methods of calculating streamribbons (firstly using two adjacent streamlines and secondly by directly relating twist to angular velocity in the manner of Fig. 7.7) is the topic of Pagendarm and Post [43]. Visualization of flows is often as much a matter of knowing what to leave out as what to put in, and the simplification of vector field representations is discussed by Telea and van Wijk [53].

Dealing with dense representation approaches, spot noise is described by van Wijk [57] and line integral convolution by Cabral and Leedom [12]. These two are compared by de Leeuw and van Liere [18]. van Wijk [59] describes the generation of flow textures at interactive framerates by the advection of images using a mesh distorted according to the flow. Reference [59] deals with 2D domains, whilst Telea and van Wijk [54] describe the extension of the method to 3D.

References

1. Brodlie KW (ed.) (1992) Visualization techniques. In: Brodlie KW, Carpenter LA, Earnshaw RA, Gallop JR, Hubbold RJ, Mumford AM, Osland CD, Quarendon P (eds.) Scientific visualization: Techniques and applications. Springer, Berlin Heidelberg New York.
2. Brodlie KW (1993) A classification scheme for scientific visualization. In: Earnshaw RA, Watson D (eds.) Animation and Scientific Visualization: Tools and applications. Academic Press, London San Diego.
3. Brodlie KW (1995) Nuclear Instruments and Methods in Physics Research A 354:104–111.
4. Brodlie KW, Asim MR, Unsworth K (2005) Computer Graphics Forum 24(4):809–820.
5. Brodlie KW, Duce DA, Gallop JR, Sagar M, Walton JPRB, Wood JD (2004) Visualization in gcid computing environments. In: Rushmeier H, Turk G, van Wijk JJ (eds.) Proceedings of IEEE Visualization 2004 Conference. IEEE Computer Society Press.
6. Brodlie KW, Duce DA, Gallop JR, Walton JPRB, Wood JD (2004) Computer Graphics Forum 23(2):223–251.
7. Brodlie KW, Mashwama P (1997) Controlled interpolation for scientific visualization. In: Nielson GM, Hagen H, Müller H (eds.) Scientific Visualization: Overviews, Methodologies, Techniques. IEEE Computer Society Press.
8. Brodlie K, Poon A, Wright H, Brankin L, Banecki G, Gay A (1993) GRASPARC: A problem solving environment integrating computation and visualization. In: Bergeron D, Nielson GM (eds.) Proceedings of IEEE Visualization 1993 Conference. IEEE Computer Society Press.
9. Brodlie K, Wood JD (2001) Computer Graphics Forum 20(2):125–148.
10. Butler DM, Pendley MH (1989) Computers in Physics 3(5):45–51.
11. Bunks C (1996) Grokking the GIMP. New Riders [Available online: gug. sunsite.dk/docs/Grokking-the-GIMP-v1.0/].
12. Cabral B, Leedom L. (1993) Imaging vector fields using line integral convolution. In: Kajiya JT, Cox D (eds.) Proceedings ACM SIGGRAPH 93. ACM Press, New York.
13. Cameron G (ed.) (1995) Computer Graphics 29(2).
14. Chen M, Kaufman AE, Yagel R (eds.) (2000) Volume Graphics. Springer-Verlag, London.

15. Collins BM (1993) Data visualization – has it all been seen before? In: Earn-shaw RA, Watson D (eds.) Animation and Scientific Visualization: Tools and applications. Academic Press, London San Diego.
16. Cottafava G, Le Moli G (1969) Communications of the ACM 12(7):386–391.
17. Crane CM (1972) Computer Journal 15:382–384.
18. de Leeuw W, van Liere R (1998) Comparing LIC and spot noise. In: Ebert D, Hagen H, Rushmeier H (eds.) Proceedings of IEEE Visualization 1998 Confer-ence. IEEE Computer Society Press.
19. Foster I, Kesselman C (eds.) (2003) Grid 2: Blueprint for a new computing infrastructure. Morgan Kaufman.
20. Gallop JR (1994) State of the art in visualization software. In: Hearnshaw HM, Unwin DJ (eds.) Visualization in Geographical Information Systems. Wiley, Chichester UK.
21. Gregory RL (1998) Eye and brain: The psychology of seeing. 5th ed. Oxford University Press.
22. Grimes J (1996) On the failure to detect changes in scenes across saccades. In: Akins K (ed.) Perception. Oxford University Press, New York.
23. Haber RB (1990) Computing Systems in Engineering 1(1):37–50.
24. Haber RB, Lucas B, Collins N (1991) A data model for scientific visualization with provisions for regular and irregular grids. In: Nielson GM, Rosenblum LJ (eds.) Proceedings of IEEE Visualization 1991 Conference. IEEE Computer Society Press.
25. Haber RB, McNabb DA (1990) Visualization idioms: A conceptual model for scientific visualization systems. In: Nielson GM, Shriver B, Rosenblum LJ (eds.) Visualization in Scientific Computing. IEEE, New York.
26. Hansen CD, Johnson CR (eds.) (2005) The Visualization Handbook. Elsevier, Oxford.
27. Hearn D, Baker MP (2004) Computer graphics with OpenGL. 3rd ed. Pearson Prentice Hall.
28. Hultquist JPM (1992) Constructing stream surfaces in steady 3D vector fields. In: Kaufman A, Nielson GM (eds.) Proceedings of IEEE Visualization 1992 Conference. IEEE Computer Society Press.
29. Ihaka   R   (2003)   Colour   me...carefully   [Available   online: www.stat.auckland.ac.nz/~ihaka/color-talk.pdf].
30. Kerlick GD, Kirby E (1993) Towards interactive steering, visualization and animation of unsteady finite element simulations. In: Bergeron D, Nielson GM (eds.) Proceedings of IEEE Visualization 1993 Conference. IEEE Computer Society Press.
31. Lane DA (1997) Scientific visualization of large-scale unsteady fluid flows. In: Nielson GM, Hagen H, Müller H (eds.) Scientific Visualization: Overviews, Methodologies, Techniques. IEEE Computer Society Press.
32. Laramee RS, Hauser H, Doleisch H, Vrolijk B, Post FH, Weiskopf D (2004) Computer Graphics Forum 23(2):203–221.
33. Levoy M (1988) IEEE Computer Graphics and Applications 8(3):29–37.
34. Levoy M (1990) ACM Transactions on Graphics 9(3):245–261.
35. Liu Z, Moorhead RJ (2005) IEEE Transactions on Visualization and Computer Graphics 11(2):113–125.
36. Lorensen WE, Cline HE (1987) Computer Graphics 21(4):163–169.
37. Marshall R, Kempf J, Dyer S, Yen C (1990) Computer Graphics 24(2):89-97.

38. McCormick B, DeFanti TA, Brown MD (1987) Computer Graphics 21(6).
39. Montag ED (2005) Color gamut mapping [Available online: www.cis.rit.edu/people/faculty/montag].
40. Mueller K, Möller T, Crawfis R (1999) Splatting without the blur. In: Ebert D, Gross M, Hamann B (eds.) Proceedings of IEEE Visualization 1999 Conference. IEEE Computer Society Press.
41. Nielson GM (1997) Tools for triangulations and tetrahedrizations and constructing functions defined over them. In: Nielson GM, Hagen H, Müller H (eds.) Scientific Visualization: Overviews, Methodologies, Techniques. IEEE Computer Society Press.
42. Nielson GM, Hamann B (1991) The asymptotic decider: Resolving the ambiguity in marching cubes. In: Nielson GM, Rosenblum L (eds.) Proceedings of IEEE Visualization 1991 Conference. IEEE Computer Society Press.
43. Pagendarm H-G, Post FH (1997) Studies in comparative visualization of flow features. In: Nielson GM, Hagen H, Müller H (eds.) Scientific Visualization: Overviews, Methodologies, Techniques. IEEE Computer Society Press.
44. Pickles SM, Blake RJ, Boghosian BM, Brooke JM, Chin J, Clarke PEL, Coveney PV, Gonzlez-Segredo N, Haines R, Harting J, Harvey M, Jones MAS, McKeown M, Pinning RL, Porter AR, Roy K, Riding M (2004) The TeraGyroid experiment. In: Hinke T, Cox SJ, Hood RT, Towns J (eds.) Workshop on Case Studies on Grid Applications. GGF10.
45. Post FH, van Wijk JJ (1994) Visual representation of vector fields: Recent developments and research directions. In: Rosenblum L, Earnshaw RA, Encarnacao J, Hagen H, Kaufman A, Klimenko S, Nielson GM, Post FH, Thalmann D (eds.) Scientific visualization: Advances and Challenges. Academic Press.
46. Powell MJD, Sabin MA (1977) ACM Transactions on Mathematical Software 3(4):316–325.
47. Poynton C (2000) Frequently-Asked Questions about Color [Available online: www.poynton.com/ColorFAQ.html].
48. Preusser A (1989) ACM Transactions on Mathematical Software 15(1):79–89.
49. Rasche K, Geist R, Westall J (2005) Computer Graphics Forum 24(3):423–432.
50. Robertson PK (1988) IEEE Computer Graphics and Applications 8(5):50–64.
51. Smith AR (1978) Computer Graphics 12(3):12–19.
52. Snyder WV (1978) ACM Transactions on Mathematical Software 4(3):290–294.
53. Telea A, van Wijk JJ (1999) Simplified representation of vector fields. In: Ebert D, Gross M, Hamann B (eds.) Proceedings of IEEE Visualization 1999 Conference. IEEE Computer Society Press.
54. Telea A, van Wijk JJ (2003) 3D IBFV: Hardware-accelerated 3D flow visualization. In: Moorhead R, Turk G, van Wijk JJ (eds.) Proceedings of IEEE Visualization 2003 Conference. IEEE Computer Society Press.
55. Tufte ER (2001) Visual Display of Quantitative Information. Graphics Press, USA.
56. Upson C, Faulhaber T Jr, Kamins D, Laidlaw D, Schlegel D, Vroom J, Gurwitz R, van Dam A (1989) IEEE Computer Graphics and Applications 9(4):30–42.
57. van Wijk JJ (1991) Computer Graphics, 25(4):309-318.
58. van Wijk JJ (1993) Implicit stream surfaces. In: Bergeron D, Nielson GM (eds.) Proceedings of IEEE Visualization 1993 Conference. IEEE Computer Society Press.
59. van Wijk JJ (2002) ACM Transactions on Graphics 21(3):745–754.

60. van Wijk JJ, van Liere R (1997) An environment for computational steering. In: Nielson GM, Hagen H, Müller H (eds.) Scientific Visualization: Overviews, Methodologies, Techniques. IEEE Computer Society Press.

61. Walton JPRB (2005) NAG's IRIS Explorer. In: Hansen CD, Johnson CR (eds.) The Visualization Handbook. Elsevier, Oxford [Available online: www.nag.co.uk/doc/TechRep/Pdf/tr2_03.pdf].

62. Weiskopf D, Erlebacher G (2005) Overview of flow visualization. In: Hansen CD, Johnson CR (eds.) The Visualization Handbook. Elsevier, Oxford.

63. Westover L (1990) Computer Graphics 24(4):367–376.

64. Wikipedia (2005) Beta movement [Available online: en.wikipedia.org/wiki/Beta_movement].

65. Wikipedia (2005) Cone cells [Available online: en.wikipedia.org/wiki/Cone_cells].

66. Wilhelms J, Van Gelder A (1990) Computer Graphics, 24(5):79–86.

67. Wood JD (1998) Collaborative Visualization. PhD Thesis, University of Leeds, UK [Available online: www.comp.leeds.ac.uk/jason/].

68. Wright H (2004) Putting visualization first in computational steering. In: Cox SJ (ed.) Proceedings of All Hands 2004. EPSRC Sept 2004 [Available online: www.allhands.org.uk/2004/proceedings/papers/139.pdf].

69. Zöckler M, Stalling D, Hege H-C (1996) Interactive visualization of 3D-vector fields using illuminated streamlines. In: Nielson GM, Yagel R (eds.) Proceedings of IEEE Visualization 1996 Conference. IEEE Computer Society Press.

Solutions

Chapter 2

2.1 Nominal data commonly found in the press includes profits recorded by company name, gross national product per country, votes cast by political party allegiance, sunshine hours by city.

Shares data versus time, as discussed in the chapter, is one that is frequently plotted as a continuum even if the figures represent averages over some period. Other quantities that are frequently similarly mistreated are average earnings, average prices, average productivity. Data that is often collected in terms of a numerical range rather than by means of a specific quantity includes a person's age, her earnings, days off sick, visits to the doctor, number of pets, number in household. No data points that have been gathered in this way should be connected together into a line graph.

2.2 Objects in an ordinary office: computer mouse with a satin surface shows a highlight and shading which indicate it is smoothly curved at the rear and an abrupt change in shading at the front indicating an edge; paperknife that is shiny and has a very narrow highlight when turned, showing it is reasonably sharp; fax machine has a sharp feature on the front which is only evident by touch, due to its matte surface which is currently in shade.

Chapter 4

4.1 The streetlamp emits a monochromatic light whose frequency is such that it excites both the middle- and long-wavelength cone cells. The combined signals from these cells are interpreted as seeing the colour yellow. On the computer monitor, two different phosphors emit light at two different frequencies, which each excite the middle- and long-wavelength systems but to different degrees. The combined signals are once again interpreted as seeing the colour yellow. The two sensations are indistinguishable even though they arise from intrinsically different stimuli.

4.2 The fully saturated colours lie on the three cube faces that meet at the black point. The full-value colours lie on the three cube faces that meet at the white point.

Yellow and magenta are secondary colours each made up of two primaries: yellow is composed of red and green whilst magenta is composed of red and blue. Dark yellow is therefore $(1, 1, 0)/2 + (0, 0, 0)/2 = (0.5, 0.5, 0)$ and pale magenta is $(1, 0, 1)/2 + (1, 1, 1)/2 = (1, 0.5, 1)$. When estimating the coordinates of a point in the RGB cube, you might find it useful to orient the positive x-axis (i.e., red) to run left-to-right, the positive y-axis (i.e., green) to run bottom-to-top, and the positive z-axis (blue) to come towards you out of the screen.

4.3 The two renderings differ only in the shade of grey used in their backgrounds. When the luminance of the background is roughly the same as the brighter, yellow-coloured arrows, then the blue ones are the more noticeable and the flow appears predominantly upwards. With a darker background the situation is reversed and the flow appears predominantly downwards because the yellow arrows stand out. In fact, the contributions of all the arrows roughly cancel each other out and the flow is neither predominantly upwards nor downwards. In this example the user's insight into his data could be severely compromised by such an arbitrary choice as the grey of the background used.

The effect can be confirmed as having nothing to do with the data by altering the grey background level on just one of the renderings. It should be possible to find two points either side of mid-grey – one where the yellow arrows virtually disappear and the other where the blue ones are nearly invisible. The distance between these two points represents the extent of the luminance imbalance across the colour map employed. Above and below these points, both sets of arrows can be distinguished but on a dark background the blue is less noticeable and on a light background the yellow fails to stand out. Only one background shade of mid-grey renders both sets equally visible, as they should be.

4.4 Recall that the fully saturated colours lie on the three cube faces that meet at the black point and the full-value colours lie on the three cube faces that meet at the white point. Sky blue and orange each lie on an edge that is shared between a full-saturation face and a full-value face; therefore, they both have $S = 1$ and $V = 1$.

At the green end of the green-magenta colour map the green component can be estimated at about two-thirds, or 0.67. Since this is a linear mapping through the midpoint $G = 0.5$, the green component at the opposite end must be as far below 0.5 as 0.67 is above, i.e., at 0.33. The base hue at this opposite end is magenta, i.e., $R = 1$, $B = 1$. The endpoints are therefore $(0, 0.67, 0)$ and $(1, 0.33, 1)$ which yield luminances of $0.7152 \times 0.67 = 0.48$

and $0.2126 \times 1 + 0.7152 \times 0.33 + 0.0722 \times 1 = 0.52$, respectively. The small deviation from 0.5 is due to the approximate nature of the estimating process. Note also that these endpoint colours are complementary, as they must be when any point on the RGB cube is reflected through the body diagonal (see Sect. 4.3.1).

A colour map linking yellow and blue involves estimating RGB values on the face of the cube, which is difficult to do accurately. In this case the endpoint colours are best calculated from the luminance equation, (4.1). We can also note for simplification that for any shade of yellow $R = G$, hence at the yellow end $0.2126 \times R + 0.7152 \times G = 0.9278 \times R = 0.5$ i.e., $R = G = 0.539$. Using the requirement for complementarity the endpoint colours are therefore $(0.539, 0.539, 0)$ and $(0.461, 0.461, 1)$. Our perceptual nonlinearity is easy to see in this result: a tiny variation across the scale in yellow is balancing the maximum possible variation in blue component. However, reducing the value of yellow to this extent makes for such a dark shade that the original hue is difficult to discern. Contrast this colour map with the fully saturated, full-value endpoints of the sky blue-orange one, but where the colours were nonetheless equiluminant.

Using this colour map in the software of problem 4.3 you should find that all the arrows are either equally hard (when the luminance of the background is about one-half) or equally easy (against a rather different grey) to see. The situation is the converse of that in the earlier problem, since now only one background shade, mid-grey, renders the visualization useless (though not untruthful), whilst all the other shades that may be chosen will make both sets of arrows more or less, but nonetheless equally, visible.

Chapter 5

5.1 Figures 2.1 to 2.3 are all 1D nominal scalar data. Figure 2.4 is 1D ordinal, and Fig. 2.5 is 2D ordinal, scalar data. Figure 2.6 is 2D nominal scalar data and Fig. 2.7, being a slice, has reduced this to 1D nominal scalar data. Figures 2.8 and 2.9 are both 1D nominal scalar data. Figures 2.10 to 2.12 are all 2D ordinal scalar data. Figure 2.13 is 2D ordinal scalar data that is also time-varying. Figure 2.14 is 3D ordinal scalar data. Figures 2.15 and 2.17 are both 1D ordinal scalar data that is discontinuous. Figure 2.16 has the same data classification as Figs. 2.1 to 2.3. Figures 2.18 and 2.19 are 1D aggregated scalar data. Figure 2.20 is 1D ordinal scalar data that is continuous but has been interpolated incorrectly. Figure 2.21 is 1D ordinal scalar data.

Figure 3.3 is 1D ordinal scalar data and Fig. 3.4 is 2D ordinal scalar data.

Table 5.1 and Fig. 5.1 are 1D ordinal scalar data. Figure 5.3 is 1D ordinal multiple scalar data. Figures 5.4 and 5.5 interpret this same data as 1D ordinal but vector type.

5.2 The two independent variables are latitude and longitude, needed to pin-point a two-dimensional position, whilst the dependent variable is the height of the terrain at that position. This data is ordinal. A rambler's map of the countryside will usually use contours, since it is important to judge the lay of the land locally and quite accurately in order to orient oneself and plan a route. In an atlas it is more common to see colour used. By contrast this can give an overview of a much larger area but the colour bands used span large ranges of the heights. Two or three hues may be used to good effect – progressively purer blue for deeper seas; green blending to orange for low to medium altitude land; finally decreasing saturation towards white to evoke the snow-tipped peaks of the highest parts.

5.3 Latitude and longitude are again the independent variables and again this data is ordinal. Isobars, literally lines of "same weight", connect those points where the dependent variable, the pressure of the air, is the same. In Table 5.2 this technique is called a contour plot; another generic name would be "isoline".

5.4 The wind speed and direction of the air comprises one vector dependent variable. The temperature of the air is a second, scalar dependent variable that can be added to the arrow plot in the form of colour.

Chapter 6

6.1 The upper plot generates four triangles per rectangular cell and draws the straight line contours within these triangles. The middle plot shows contours drawn as smooth curves within each rectangular cell. The lower contours are straight lines drawn over a mesh comprising only two triangles per rectangular cell. The first two plots follow faithfully the particular model chosen for the data, but differ in appearance because the two models are different. In the third the contours follow the planar model fitted to each triangle, but the overall arrangement is insufficient. The bottom plot thus loses its mirror symmetry, because the ambiguities involving the green contour are resolved correctly on the right-hand side but incorrectly on the left. Had the triangulation been chosen with diagonals in the opposite sense, the plot would have been correct on its left-hand side and incorrect on the right. The problem has arisen because the values were converted at the filter stage of the visualization pipeline into a data structure intended for scattered points. Because of the underlying regularity of this gridded data, this choice later proves inappropriate.

6.2 The first 'surface view' has been produced with physically flat geometry but normals applied that would result from the equivalent, displaced surface. When viewed from a near-overhead position and rotated slightly the apparent shading of the facets gives the fairly convincing impression that the geometry is nonplanar; only a very oblique viewing angle reveals this is not in fact the case. The second surface, conversely, is physically nonplanar but has normals applicable to planar geometry. This arrangement reveals almost nothing, showing how essential shading is to understanding the variation of data across the domain.

6.3 A visual comparison shows the green, yellow, and orange features respectively are approximately equivalent to isosurfaces with threshold values 4.5, 1.3, and 0.2.

6.4 Rendering semi-transparent isosurfaces is reminiscent of the volume rendered visualization. The classification of data for the latter was arranged to have marked steps in transparency to pick out boundaries, equivalent to the particular threshold values found in Prob. 6.3.

If the visualization is to appear in a book or traditional journal, then the animated technique is clearly not viable. If the medium is interactive, either variant might be used, though the animated one probably will take longer to understand. Balanced against this is the ability of the animated variant to show all the threshold values, whereas the other can only show a small number of surfaces. Detail between the chosen thresholds, such as when the different parts of the surface separate, will be lost.

Chapter 7

7.1 The z component of the vector at each point is a function of height, with the actual value scaled according to the parameter α. Increasing α has the effect of proportionately increasing the z component, with the exception of those points with $z = 0$, so the streamline appears to spiral less tightly for larger α. When nearest neighbour interpolation is selected for a seed position close to $z = 0$, the streamline goes round and round in circles on the base plane because the particle never receives any upward motion. This is not the case for trilinear interpolation because the blending of the zero z component with the next (albeit small) nonzero value eventually moves the particle off the base. Both nearest neighbour and trilinear interpolation produce a spiral for a seed position with $z > 0$, but the radius of the spiral (incorrrectly) spreads out a little when nearest neighbour interpolation is selected.

7.2 The techniques in use are a streamline and line integral convolution (a flow texture). The visualization is an approximation because the flow texture technique has been applied on a slice of the domain by neglecting the vector component orthogonal to the plane. In effect, the vectors have been projected onto the plane before having the flow texture applied. The approximation is modest on the outer edges of the plane where the small pitch of the streamline shows that the vector component normal to the plane is small. The approximation appears more significant towards the centre of the plane.

Useful Information

Web Sites

www.accusoft.com AccuSoft Corporation

www.allhands.org.uk/archive/index.html UK e-Science All Hands Archive

www.avs.com Advanced Visual Systems

www.hlrs.de High Performance Computing Centre, Stuttgart

www.kitware.com Kitware, Inc.

www.mc.com Mercury Computer Systems, Inc

www.m-w.com Merriam-Webster online dictionary and thesaurus

www.nag.co.uk Numerical Algorithms Group Ltd.

www.opendx.org Open Visualization Data Explorer

www.paraview.org Parallel Visualization Application

www.rcuk.ac.uk/escience/ UK Research Councils' e-Science programme

www.rsinc.com Research Systems, Inc.

www.sci.utah.edu SCI Institute, University of Utah

www.tcl.tk Tcl developer exchange

www.tecplot.com Tecplot, Inc.

www.vischeck.com Anomalous colour vision simulator

www.visenso.de Visual Engineering Solutions, GmbH

www.vni.com Visual Numerics, Inc.

www.w3.org W3C World Wide Web Consortium

www.web3d.org Web3D Consortium, including information on X3D

wikipedia.org Wikipedia, The Free Encyclopedia

Abbreviations

AM Amplitude Modulation

apE application production Environment

AVO Abstract Visualization Object

AVS Application Visualization System (the product); Advanced Visual Systems (the company)

CFD Computational Fluid Dynamics

CIE Commission Internationale de l'Eclairage (trans. International Commission on Illumination)

COVISE COllaborative VIsualization and Simulation Environment

CRT Cathode Ray Tube

CT Computed Tomograph

FM Frequency Modulation

GCSE General Certificate of Secondary Education

GUI Graphical User Interface

HLRS High Performance Computing Center, Stuttgart

HLS Hue, Lightness, and Saturation (colour model)

HSV Hue, Saturation, and Value (colour model)

IBFV Image-based Flow Visualization

IBM International Business Machines

IDL Interactive Data Language

LCD Liquid Crystal Display

LIC Line Integral Convolution

MVE Modular Visualization Environment

NAG Numerical Algorithms Group

NSF National Science Foundation

OpenDX Open Visualization Data Explorer

OSGP Ohio Supercomputer Graphics Project

ParaView Parallel Visualization Application

RGB Red, Green, and Blue (colour model)

SCI Scientific Computing and Imaging

SGI Silicon Graphics, Inc

SPECT Single-Photon Emission Computed Tomograph

Tcl Tool Command Language

Tk as in Tcl/Tk: GUI toolkit for Tcl

URL Uniform Resource Locator

ViSC Visualization in Scientific Computing

VISENSO VISual ENgineering SOlutions

VRML Virtual Reality Modelling Language

VTK The Visualization Toolkit

X3D XML-enabled 3D file format to succeed VRML

XML eXtensible Markup Language

YAC Yet-Another-COVISE

Glossary

Abstract visualization object. An imaginary object with attributes such as size, colour, transparency, texture, and so on. Data is mapped to these attributes in order to represent it visually.

Additive model. An additive colour model describes the production of colour by combining lights of various primary colours. Both RGB and HSV are additive models of colour (cf. subtractive model).

Aggregated data. Occurs where a range of values in the data domain contribute to a single value for the dependent variable that is applicable across the whole of that range.

Analytical solution. Mathematical formulation of the solution to a problem (cf. discretisation, numerical solution).

Application builder. In visualization, is synonymous with modular visualization environment.

Auditory display. Computer system output that varies pitch, loudness, and possibly timbre (character) of sound in order to convey meaning.

Basis functions. A weighted sum of basis functions interpolates the values of a variable within the range of the functions' definition. For example, $f(x) = f_0 \times (1 - x) + f_1 \times x$ interpolates linearly between f_0 and f_1 for x in the range 0 to 1. The functions $1 - x$ and x are said to be basis functions.

Batch computing. A mode of working where a collection of commands and data are first gathered together, submitted to a computer and the results retrieved later. In computational science, is in the opposite sense to computational steering.

Beta movement. A sense of motion induced by seeing a sequence of slightly different still images in rapid succession.

Body-fitted mesh. See curvilinear grid.

Cartesian coordinate system. Coordinates defined on a set of two or three orthogonal axes (cf. polar coordinate system).

Client-server architecture. An arrangement of separate, networked processes whereby client programs make requests of server programs, which in turn generate and send back replies.

Co-linear. Points are co-linear if they can be connected by a single straight line.

Co-planar. Points are co-planar if arranged so as all to sit on one plane. Any two, and possibly more, co-planar points will also be co-linear.

Collaborative visualization. Visualization by a group of users, usually geographically separated, working together on a shared problem. Can involve synchronisation of a set of pipelines running locally, or include a degree of distributed visualization, or a combination of both.

Colour gamut. The subset of all visible colours that a device can reproduce.

Colour map. A colour look-up table made by combining a line or curve in some colour space with a definition of how data is distributed along it.

Complementary colours. In an additive model, colours are said to be complementary if they sum to white.

Computational science. Science accomplished using computers, as distinct from the science or study of computers themselves.

Computed tomograph. Investigation technique whereby X-rays are passed through a subject from various directions and the emerging rays are collected by sensitive detectors, rather than film. A computer reconstructs each examined cross-section in grid-wise fashion in order to build up a three-dimensional density map.

Computational steering. An investigative paradigm where the parameters of a running simulation can be altered by an experimenter according to what is currently seen in the visualization of the results.

Cone cell. Receptor in the retina that is preferentially sensitive to short-, medium- or long-wavelength light.

Continuity. A function is said to be C^0 continuous if its data values "join on" across piecewise elements, C^1 continuous if its first derivatives match, and C^2 continuous when its second derivatives correspond.

Critical fusion frequency, or flicker fusion frequency. The frequency at which a flashing light will appear continuous to an observer, partly due to the chemical process of light detection that takes place in the retina.

Curvilinear grid. Conceptually, curvilinear grids begin life as rectilinear grids but are then distorted to fit the problem being considered. A common use is as a body-fitted mesh, whose boundary outlines some object of interest in the simulation. Body-fitted meshes can also result from a triangulation or tetrahedrisation of scattered data.

Data domain. The portion of (usually) space and/or time that is spanned by the independent variable(s). For example, the phrase "1D domain" indicates a problem with one independent variable.

Dataflow program. An application composed of a number of asynchronous processes connected together in a directed graph, the connections carrying data streams that are operated on by the processes.

Dependent variable. The variables of a problem whose values are calculated or measured once particular values(s) of the independent variable have been decided upon. Often, though not exclusively, are mapped to height or colour in a visualization.

Deuteranope. Person with colour vision deficiency stemming from the middle-wavelength or 'green' receptor system.

Diffuse reflection. Light reflected equally in all directions as from a matte surface (cf. specular reflection).

Directed acyclic graph. A set of nodes and their connections that can only be traversed in one direction and where no sequence of connections forms a closed loop. A directed graph relaxes this last condition.

Discretisation. Computational science often sets out with a mathematical formulation of a problem but typically the equations cannot be solved analytically over the whole domain. Discretisation is the process of breaking down into smaller chunks that can be solved numerically.

Distributed visualization. A mode of working where some parts of the visualization pipeline are hosted remotely from the user observing the results.

Dual graph. The Delaunay triangulation is dual to the Dirichlet tessellation since the common boundaries of the latter determine the joined vertices of the former.

Extrapolation. Using a function or functions to calculate dependent variable values at places in the domain that lie beyond data points.

Fibre bundle. Cartesian product of a base space and a fibre space, respectively analogous to the independent and dependent variables of a problem. A particular set of values for the dependent variable defines a bundle cross-section. For example, data that we might plot as two line graphs drawn on the same set of axes comprises two cross-sections of a fibre bundle made up of the real number line, the fibre space, attached to every point of a 1D base space.

Filtering. In general, the transformation (often of data) from one form into another. In the dataflow model of visualization, is used to denote the transformation of raw data into derived data.

Fovea. Small but very high resolution portion of the eye's retina directly opposite the pupil.

Grid computing. Draws analogy with the electricity grid to imply pervasive and, as far as is possible transparent, access to computational resources, data sources, experimental equipment and sensors.

Haptic display. Computer system output that simulates touch and force-feedback sensations.

HSV colour model. An inverted cone-shaped (strictly, a hexcone) model constructed on axes measuring **H**ue (the colour perceived), **S**aturation (how washed out is the colour) and **V**alue (how dark is the colour).

Independent variable. The variables of a problem that define its extent, usually, though not exclusively, in space and/or time. Often, though again not exclusively, are mapped to the axes of the display and to animation.

Interpolation. Using a function or functions to calculate dependent variable values at places in the domain that lie between data points. A characteristic of an interpolating function must be that it passes through the data points.

Isoline. Lines joining function values that are the same. For 2D data is synonymous with 'contour'.

Logarithmic scale. Plotting data on a logarithmic scale involves first expressing the numbers as a base raised to a power, and then placing the number according to its power, rather than its value as we would on a linear scale. Log-linear and log-log graph paper is pre-printed at spacings that remove the need explicitly to calculate the powers. It is commonly used to show exponential and power relationships such as $y = e^{ax}$ and $y = ax^b$, since these plot as straight lines and the constants a and b can therefore easily be found.

Luminance. Photometric counterpart of the perceptual quality called brightness.

Manifold. A structure that locally appears to be of lower dimension than it does globally.

Mapping. In the dataflow model of visualization, is used to denote the allocation of certain aspects of data to control the attributes of the chosen abstract visualization object.

Mechanoreceptor. Receptor in skin that responds to an essentially mechanical stimulus such as stretching or a change in pressure.

Modular visualization environment. A visualization package consisting of an extensible library of code modules that the user connects together to build their application, usually using visual programming.

Monochromatic light. Visible radiation having a single wavelength. For example, the light from a sodium streetlamp is monochromatic and is interpreted by the viewer as having the colour yellow.

Monolith. Literally, "single stone". In computing is used to denote a program or application whose several components or facilities are gathered together into one, single unit.

Motion parallax. Apparent motion of near-field objects contrary to the observer's movement that gives a sense of depth.

Nominal data. Where the independent variable is distinguished by name and therefore there is no inherent order to the data points.

Numerical solution. See discretisation (cf. analytical solution).

Ordinal data. Where there exists an order to the data points (cf. nominal data) but values may be discontinuous (not join on) from one point to the next. If ordinal data is continuous, it will join on from one value to the next but now we must exercise care when visualizing in how we interpolate between the data points.

Orthogonal. Mutually perpendicular.

Parametric form. It is sometimes convenient to parametrise a curve rather than define it as a function of variables. For example, the sequence of points lying on the line $y = mx + c$ can be found by choosing an x and solving for y. Alternatively the relationship can be parametrised as two equations in t, i.e. $(y = mt + c; x = t)$. Conceptually we fix t as a distance along the line and solve for both x and y. Another example: the parametric form of a circle $x^2 + y^2 = r^2$ is $(x = r\cos\theta; y = r\sin\theta)$. The parameter θ is the angle subtended by the radius passing through point (x, y) on the circle.

Perceptual uniformity. Perceptually uniform descriptions of colour aim to make equal-sized steps within the colour space correspond with equal changes in perceptual response.

Perceptualisation. Counterpart of visualization that uses other than the visual sense to give insight into data. May include auditory display and haptic display.

Perspective view. An object or scene rendered so that distant objects seem smaller and parallel lines converge to a vanishing point.

Polar coordinate system. Three-dimensional cylindrical polar coordinates are defined in terms of an angle within a plane containing the origin, a radial distance from the origin within this plane, and a perpendicular distance from this plane. Two-dimensional polar coordinates dispense with the perpendicular measure. Spherical polar coordinates are defined in terms of an angle within a plane containing the origin, an angle from a line perpendicular to this plane and a radial distance from the origin.

Polygon. Many-sided closed shape.

Polyhedron. Many-faceted closed volume built by connecting polygons edge-to-edge.

Polyline. Multisegmented line comprising a list of the segments' endpoints.

Position vector. The position vector $\mathbf{r}$ of a point $P(x, y, z)$ is $\mathbf{r} = x\mathbf{x} + y\mathbf{y} + z\mathbf{z}$ where $\mathbf{x}$, $\mathbf{y}$ and $\mathbf{z}$ are vectors of length 1 defining P's coordinate system.

Program library. A convenient way to re-use software, whereby commonly needed functionality is kept separate and described at a high level by means of an interface. The programmer uses the software by assigning values to the parameters in the interface, but remains unaware of its implementation details.

Protanope. Person with colour vision deficiency stemming from the long-wavelength or 'red' receptor system.

RGB colour model. A cube-shaped model constructed on axes measuring the contribution of **R**ed, **G**reen, and **B**lue primaries to a resulting mixture colour.

Radian. The angle between two radii of a circle of radius r that cuts off on its circumference an arc of length r. Since the circumference of a circle is $2\pi r$ it follows that one complete revolution comprises 2π radian.

Rendering. In visualization, the realisation of the abstract visualization object as an image on the chosen display device.

Retina. The light-sensitive surface covering the interior of the eye.

Saccades. Reflexive eye movements that bring a particular portion of the field of view onto the eye's fovea and during which vision is suppressed.

Saddle. Data whose cross-section is valley-shaped in one direction and hill-shaped in another. The particular place where locally the cross-section with the highest valley intersects that with the lowest hill is the saddle point itself.

Scalar. An entity that can be described by a single number.

Shade. Increasing the amount of black in a colour gives rise to progressively darker shades.

Slicing. Reducing the dimension of the independent variable space whilst leaving the dependent variable space unchanged (cf. stacking).

Specular reflection. Light reflected in a particular direction giving the spot or streak of light (specular highlight) that is characteristic of a shiny surface (cf. diffuse reflection).

Stacking. (1) Composition of a set of lower-dimensional independent variable spaces into a single higher-dimensional space. A requirement is that the constituent spaces must all involve the same dependent variable(s) (cf. slicing). (2) Concatenation of bars in a chart or the plotting of one variable on the rising baseline of preceding one(s), in order to show multiple scalar dependent variables simultaneously.

Subtractive model. A subtractive colour model describes the production of colour by selective absorption from incident light composed of a mixture of colours (cf. additive model).

Surface normal. A vector perpendicular to the surface at its point of attachment.

Surface shading. Flat shading of (for example) a triangle mesh uses the angle between the surface normal of each facet and a directional light source in order to calculate how much light is reflected in the viewing direction. This in turn determines how bright the whole of that particular surface triangle should appear. Smooth shading first constructs vertex normals, often by averaging the surface normals of each triangle around the vertex. For any one triangle, each vertex normal will typically point in a different direction, giving a different apparent brightness for the same light source. These different values are then interpolated across the triangle.

Taxonomy. The science of classification.

Tessellation. A space-filling collection of polygons. From the Latin *tesserae* meaning tiles.

Tiling. The practice of arranging a sequence of visualizations to form a single display.

Tint. Decreasing the amount of white in a colour gives rise to progressively purer tints.

Tristimulus theory. A theory of colour vision that proposes three types of colour receptor, each preferentially sensitive to light of a particular wavelength.

Tritanope. Person with colour vision deficiency stemming from the short-wavelength or 'blue' receptor system.

Trompe l'oeil. An art form whereby planar drawings, pictures, and friezes are specifically executed so as to fool the observer into thinking the subject is a tangible, three-dimensional artefact. Examples include a flat ceiling painted to mimic a domed interior, or apartment 'balconies' that do not really project from the wall that 'supports' them. Characteristically there may be a particular combination of viewing position and incident light direction that renders the *trompe l'oeil* virtually indistinguishable from the real thing.

Turnkey visualizer. A type of visualization program that works without first requiring any program construction or customisation phase.

Vector. An entity that consists of a magnitude (a scalar quantity) and a direction defined according to some coordinate system.

Vertex. In computer graphics, a mesh is made up of vertices (nodes) connected by lines (edges). In visualization, data is commonly associated with vertices or the cells enclosed by vertices and their connecting lines.

Virtual reality modelling language. Together with its successor X3D, VRML provides a file format that permits description of three-dimensional objects and scenes. Used to convey geometry content over the World Wide Web.

Visual programming. A paradigm whereby the user interactively connects together functional components within a visual workspace, in order to construct a working program.

Index

"function of" notation, 57
2D bar chart, 10, 73, 121
2D histogram, 75

abstract visualization object, 28, 57, 65, 69, 121
AccuSoft, 35
additive colour model, 40, 42
Advanced Visual Systems, 35
aggregated data, 20, 64
ambiguity, 84, 96, 123
amira, 35, 119
animation, 17, 18, 66, 67, 92, 121
anomalous colour vision, 38, 53, 119, 120
anomalous trichromacy, 120
apE, 33
application builder, 33
arrow plot, 64, 104
auditory display, 66
AVS, 33, 35
AVS/Express, 35, 119

bar chart, 20, 64, 69
basis functions, 118
beta movement, 17, 117
body-fitted mesh, 90
bounded region plot, 76
brightness, 50, 120

C++, 34
Cartesian coordinates, 59, 103
classification, 98, 101
clustering, 69, 73

collaborative visualization, 32, 118
colour gamut, 41
colour mapping, 46
colour perception, 38
colour vision deficiency, 38, 53, 119, 120
complementary colours, 40
compositing, 98, 123
computational steering, 30, 118
cones, 38, 46, 50, 53, 119
contour plot, 14, 64, 66, 81, 92, 121, 122
COVISE, 35
critical fusion frequency, 17

data domain, 58, 121
data enrichment, 28
data referencing, 35
dataflow model, 28, 118
degrees of freedom, 65, 69
Delaunay triangulation, 80, 85, 122
dependent variable, 55, 60, 121
deuter-anope,-anopia,-anomaly, 120
dichromacy, 120
directed acyclic graph, 28
Dirichlet tessellation, 80
discontinuous data, 20, 64, 77
discrete solution, 58, 122
distortion, 12, 14
distributed visualization, 31, 118
drag-and-drop, 33

electromagnetic spectrum, 37
extrapolation, 22

fibre bundle, 62, 122

filtering, 28, 118
fire hoses of data, 3, 117
flow texture, 112, 124

gradient, 85, 94, 123

haptic display, 66, 119
height-field plot, 87, 94
hidden line removal, 78
hidden surface removal, 78
higher-order interpolation, 122
histogram, 20, 72
HLRS, 35
HLS colour model, 119
HSV colour model, 42, 119, 120

IBFV, 112, 124
IBM, 33
IBM Visualization Data Explorer, 33,
    35
IDL, 34
image display, 64, 66, 76, 89, 92
image-based flow visualization, 112, 124
independent variable, 55, 58, 121
interpolation, 22, 69, 118, 122
IRIS Explorer, 33, 35, 119
isosurface, 64, 93

Khoral Research, 33
Khoros, 33, 35
Kitware, 34

LIC, 112, 124
light, 37
line graph, 22, 55, 66, 72, 118
line integral convolution, 112, 124
line of greys, 40, 42, 120
linear interpolation, 81, 89, 122
logarithmic scale, 37
luminance, 50, 120
luminance variation, 50, 52, 120

manifold, 60, 61, 66, 92, 122
mapping, 28
marching cubes, 94, 123
marching tetrahedra, 96
mathematical model, 56, 122
mechanoreceptor, 119
Mercury Computer Systems, 35
milkmaid's stool, 78

modular visualization environment, 33,
    118

NAG, 35
nearest neighbour interpolation, 89
nominal data, 20, 64, 121, 122
NSF report, 2, 117
numerical solution, 56, 58, 122

OpenDX, 35
ordinal data, 20, 64, 122
OSGP, 33

parametric form, 122
ParaView, 34, 119
pen plotter, 122
perception, 7
perceptual uniformity, 46, 50, 121
perceptualisation, 8, 66
perspective, 12, 14
phi phenomenon, 117
photopsin, 119
pie chart, 12, 70, 118
polar coordinates, 59, 103
primary colours, 40
prot-anope,-anopia,-anomaly, 120
PV-WAVE, 34

ray-casting, 98, 123
rendering, 28
Research Systems, 34
RGB colour model, 40, 120

saccades, 18, 117
saddle point, 84, 96, 123
scalars, 69, 122
scatterplot, 70, 122
SCI Institute, 35
SCIRun, 35, 119
SGI, 33
shade, 42, 52
shaded contour plot, 88
shading, 14
shared memory, 35
slicing, 62, 66, 67, 73, 74, 77, 90
spectral sensitivity, 50, 52
specular reflection, 14
splatting, 101, 123
spot noise, 112, 124
stacking, 62, 66, 69, 73, 74, 92
Stellar Computer, 33

streakline, 112
streamline, 106, 124
streamribbon, 108, 124
streamsurface, 108, 124
streamtube, 108
superimposition, 69
surface normal, 86, 94, 123
surface view, 10, 14, 66, 67, 85, 118, 121
swept polygon, 110, 124

taxonomy, 64, 122
Tecplot, 34
tetrahedrisation, 90, 122
Thiessen region, 80
Thomas Young, 40
time surface, 110
timeline, 106
tint, 42, 52
trajectory, 61, 64, 122
triangulation, 69
tristimulus theory, 38, 40
trit-anope,-anopia,-anomaly, 120

turnkey visualizer, 33

underlying model, 22, 118, 122

vectors, 103, 124
vertex normal, 86, 94, 123
VISENSO, 35
visible radiation, 37
VisiQuest, 35
Visual Numerics, 34
visual programming, 33
visualization before computers, 117
visualization command language, 34
visualization library, 34
volume render, 64, 90, 98
volume visualization, 90, 123
Voronoi diagram, 80
VRML, 31
VTK, 34, 119

YAC, 35

Printed in the United States
By Bookmasters